THE RAILROAD PASSENGER CAR

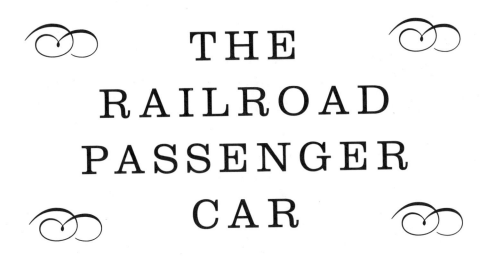

THE
RAILROAD
PASSENGER
CAR

AN ILLUSTRATED HISTORY
OF THE FIRST HUNDRED YEARS
WITH ACCOUNTS
BY CONTEMPORARY PASSENGERS

AUGUST MENCKEN

with a new introduction by Courtney B. Wilson

THE JOHNS HOPKINS UNIVERSITY PRESS
BALTIMORE AND LONDON

The Johns Hopkins University Press

2715 North Charles Street

Baltimore, Maryland 21218-4363

www.press.jhu.edu

Library of Congress Cataloging-in-Publication Data

Mencken, August, 1889–1967.

The railroad passenger car : an illustrated history of the first hundred years

with accounts by contemporary passengers /

by August Mencken ; with a new introduction by Courtney B. Wilson.

p.   cm.

Originally published: 1957.

ISBN 0-8018-6541-7 (alk. paper)

1. Railroads—United States—Passenger-cars.

2. Railroads—United States—Passenger traffic. I. Title.

TF455 .M4 2000

385´.33´0973—dc21   00-030931

A catalog record for this book is available from the British Library.

CONTENTS

PART I

. . . *The First Hundred Years*

PART II

Accounts by Contemporary Passengers

LIST OF ILLUSTRATIONS

INTRODUCTION TO THE 2000 EDITION

New works on the subject of passenger service and rail equipment appear each year. Virtually all are photographic essays on passenger coaches of particular railroads. These works interest the student of celebrated railroads and present pictorial evidence especially valuable for the scale modeler. Such books also play on our nostalgic yearning for days gone by—so much so that today we could easily fail to realize that rail travel was as revolutionary in the early nineteenth century as was space travel in the mid-twentieth century. Contemporary newspaper accounts reporting on the trial run of Peter Cooper's steam engine outside Baltimore in the summer of 1830 fussed and fumed over what effects traveling thirteen miles per hour might have on human physiology! From the first passenger coaches, which resembled little more than a wooden box on wheels, to the smooth riding and opulent Victorian palace cars at the turn of the twentieth century, the story of railroad passenger cars offers a picture of American culture, ingenuity, and capitalism at its best.

Then, trying earnestly to remain competitive in the mid-1950s, American railroads retired their great and colorful steam locomotives and, with them, the steam era's richly appointed and liveried passenger coaches. A few smoking beasts of iron and steel remained in service as mainline reserves, helping to boost coal trains up steep grades, but eventually most steam locomotives, with a few antique coaches, operated on short lines or gave birth to the phenomenon of the "tourist railway." Relying on diesel technology, regular passenger service for a time employed sleek and streamlined locomotives and matching stainless steel lightweight coaches, which coddled their fares in high style. By the time of the Eisenhower administration, heroic attempts to make passenger service profitable were failing. The building of the federally funded interstate highway system, a postwar economic boom that produced huge sales in automobiles, and the increasing success of commercial airlines spelled the doom of independent passenger railroads in the United States. The sunset of genteel rail travel—with its opulent palace cars, gourmet dining car cuisine, and immaculate passenger depots—arrived with the American achievement of personal mobility.

In the midst of this technological and economic transition, August Mencken wrote a pioneering work, *The Railroad Passenger Car*. Published by the Johns Hopkins Press in 1957, his little volume stands as a landmark in railroad history. After graduating from Baltimore's famed Polytechnic High School, Mencken spent many years as a civil engineer working in railroad construction. Retired, he became a noted author, publishing a number of historical works that covered topics as diverse as sea travel and capital punishment. Although as a writer August Mencken will always remain in the shadow of his brother Henry Louis (H. L.) Mencken, his few books explore interesting subjects in a compelling style.

At a time when hobbyists were few and the bibliography of American technological history was short, Mencken relied on a host of untapped sources to create the first comprehensive work on American railroad passenger accommodations and the patrons they served. As with many early works in other disciplines, Mencken's book lacks the kind of detailed source notes one finds in later, more refined scholarship. Despite this weakness, Mencken contributed a reliable survey of the history of technological developments emerging from passenger railroads. In groundbreaking fashion, Mencken examined the records of the United States Patent Office, early railroad journals, and newspaper accounts to present an amazing record of technological progress, one that later authors only augmented in their own studies. Mencken especially stressed how, by the mid-nineteenth century, American ingenuity had motivated the discovery of virtually all the "modern" conveniences in rail travel, including streamlining and air conditioning. He embellished his text with rare photographs and renderings gleaned from rather obscure sources, as well as patent drawings that he published for the first time. More importantly, Mencken's use of newspaper accounts, reports, journal entries, and diaries brings to the fore the human aspects of the progression of technology. In the field of railroad technological history, only this volume considers the inventive nature of railroad progress together with the technology of comfort and the people railroads served. Mencken's use of primary sources allows current readers to grasp the issues that concerned nineteenth- and early-twentieth-century railroad travelers. He helps us to understand how improvements in passenger carriages were a matter of human demand as well as pure technological innovation.

In 1978, the Johns Hopkins University Press again led the way in railroad-technology history, publishing *The American Railroad Passenger Car*, the work of John H. White, Jr., then curator of transportation at the National Museum of American History, Smithsonian Institution. Spanning the years 1830 to 1970, White's survey work (still in print) contains the scholarship, detail, and superb illustrations befitting its technical scope. It offers an example of American technological history at its very best and grew logically from Mencken's early work. Even so, the compass of White's study does not extend to the experiences of those who traveled by rail during the nineteenth and early twentieth centuries. White's annotated bibliography refers to Mencken's work as the "pioneering history of the American passenger car" and "for many years the only work available on the subject. The modest text concentrates on nineteenth-century developments. No formal documentation is offered." White cautions "not to accept the information uncritically. Reproductions of contemporary travel accounts, which occupy one half of the pages, form the most valuable portion of the book."

Mencken's work and its enduring value thus rests in its social commentary on early rail passenger travel. Mencken demonstrated that the tension between technology and human experience creates the context into which all invention must flow. He shows us all the strange, often sensible, as well as odd, things inventors designed both to pacify customers and pad the railroad owners' pockets. Mencken's book supplies the perfect introduction to a subject whose devotees increase each year. Today, visitors to the great railroad museums of the world are treated to a glimpse of passenger amenities in the preserved examples of these coaches, great and small. Although few can imagine the smoke, clatter, dirt, and danger of nineteenth-century rail travel, Mencken's research provides the contemporary description necessary to gain a full understanding of that experience.

Courtney B. Wilson
Executive Director, B&O Railroad Museum

BALTIMORE
JUNE 2000

INTRODUCTION
TO THE ORIGINAL
EDITION

With all its dangers and discomforts, the early railroad had the great advantage of speed over all other means of land transport then known, and it held that advantage until very recent years. In the first years of its existence in the United States, traveling by rail was considered a grand adventure, and as each new line was opened the surrounding population made a holiday of the event and turned out to see the first train and hear the oratory of its load of notables. As the novelty wore off, the railroads were accepted by the public as a natural phenomenon of the fast-growing country, and everyone who could find the money traveled on them. People not only traveled on them; they took a very personal and proprietory interest in them, and, as the following pages show, it was rare for an American passenger in the first years to vent a complaint. The dirt, the discomfort, and the possibility of sudden death were looked on as a small price to pay for the privilege of moving over the country at what was then a dizzy speed. While some of the English tourists of the time wrote of unpleasant experiences, they were put down as envious foreigners and received little attention.

During the railroad's first fifty years there was a constant stream of improvements in passenger cars and in the other equipment affecting the passenger. Bed cars, air conditioning, streamlining, and many other innovations introduced within the last few years were then first suggested. Some were actually tried out. But as competition among the multitude of small railroads abated, the incentive for improvement diminished, and eventually the business of devising, building, and operating luxurious passenger equipment became the monopoly of the Pullman Company. From the first it produced cars that were the equal of any in use anywhere, and under its operating system the name of Pullman became synonymous with the best in railroad travel.

In late years some of the railroads have introduced greatly improved passenger equipment to meet the competition of the airplane, the bus, and the private automobile, but on a number of them—save for changes in materials, the introduction of safety devices, and the appearance of various gadgets of which the passenger is hardly conscious—the same type of passenger equipment that was used in the 1880's is still in service.

There is an enormous literature on the railroads. All stages of their growth, from their feeble beginnings to their present decline, have been recorded many times, and there are numerous accounts of their early and continuing financial troubles. The spectacular feats of both civil and mechanical engineering that entered into their development have also been described at length. In this volume—for the first time, so far as I know—the passenger has chief attention. An attempt is made to show what his experience of railroad travel was from the earliest days: what sort of accommodation he encountered; how his safety and comfort were gradually augmented; what it cost him to travel by rail; how he reacted to it; and so on. The description begins, of necessity, with the actual lines of rail, for until they were perfected all the ensuing comforts and conveniences were quite impossible. It proceeds to an account of the development of the railroad passenger car—at first a mere adaptation of the old stagecoach, but in the end a highly refined and complicated mechanism, with an existence all its own. Its history has not been fully recorded, and there is considerable difference among authorities over this point or that. I have gone in all cases to the original patent claims, and I hope that some of the obscurities of the matter are here cleared up. At the end I append a brief note on Standard Time—a commonplace today, but something that was long in coming up and worked a revolution of the first degree.

So much for Part I. Part II is made up of extracts from narratives of railroad travel by actual passengers. I have gone through hundreds of books in search of materials, nearly all of them long out of print, and some of them existing today in but a few widely scattered copies. They are not quoted *in extenso*, but selectively, with an effort to avoid repetition. After all, most of the travelers saw the same thing. My endeavor has been to unearth those who saw it for the first time, but

I have not hesitated to add the observations of those who saw it better, if later, and describe it more vividly. The last narrative included is dated 1891, by which time railroad travel had become standardized over most parts of the United States, and the experience of one passenger had begun to be the experience of all. The great changes that have come about within the past few decades are familiar to all persons likely to read this book; moreover they are described at length in the current literature.

To the staffs of the Enoch Pratt Free Library and the Peabody Library, both of Baltimore; of the Roswell P. Flower Memorial Library, Watertown, New York; of the Bangor Public Library, Bangor, Maine; of the Municipal Reference Library, Chicago; of the library of the Association of American Railroads, Washington, D. C.; of the Railway and Locomotive Historical Society, Boston; of the Historical Society of Pennsylvania; of the corporation departments of New York, Massachusetts, Pennsylvania, and Maine, and of the U. S. Patent Office I owe thanks for valuable assistance in collecting materials. I am indebted, also, to the New York Central Railroad, the New York, New Haven and Hartford Railroad, the Pennsylvania, the Erie, the Illinois Central, the Union Pacific, the Chicago, Burlington & Quincy Railroad, the Baltimore & Ohio, and the Pullman Company for information from their files, and to my brother, the late H. L. Mencken, who helped me greatly with many suggestions.

August Mencken

BALTIMORE
JUNE 5, 1957

THE RAILROAD PASSENGER CAR

∽ PART I ∾

. . . THE FIRST HUNDRED YEARS

~ 1 ~

THE

DEVELOPMENT

OF THE

ROADBED

On a well-designed and well-maintained railroad a passenger riding in a modern car is hardly conscious of the roadbed under him. As far as he can tell from his seat, the train appears to be running on a perfectly straight and level track, and he can walk from end to end of the car with very little discomfort and no fear at all of bodily harm. If he stands at the rear end, he will see the rails coming out from under the train bright and smooth, and when they appear to change direction and form themselves into a curve, he has no sensation of the train itself changing direction. Switches and crossings are passed over without noticeable effect, and the train goes on its journey as though it were the only one running on the entire line. This is the condition on every good railroad today, but there was a time when it was not to be found anywhere. Passengers in the last century were acutely aware of the roadbed. It jarred and jolted them incessantly, and not infrequently it maimed or killed them.

The sole concern of many of the early railroad-builders was to lay track as quickly as possible and as cheaply. Some of the roads were supervised by competent engineers and were built as well as could be done at the time, but many were slapped together by promoters who employed amateurish engineers on the work, with the result that the finished roads, with their sharp curves and bumpy grades, had the appearance of roller coasters stretching across country. The curves had a violent effect on the motion of the cars, and each change in grade produced a jolt, all of which, added up, made many of the passengers ill with train sickness.

Often the track was laid with little if any ballast under the ties, and once it was in use no one seems to have paid much attention to its maintenance. In winter the track was heaved by frost, and in spring the line was buried in mud, often to the top of the rails. Derailments

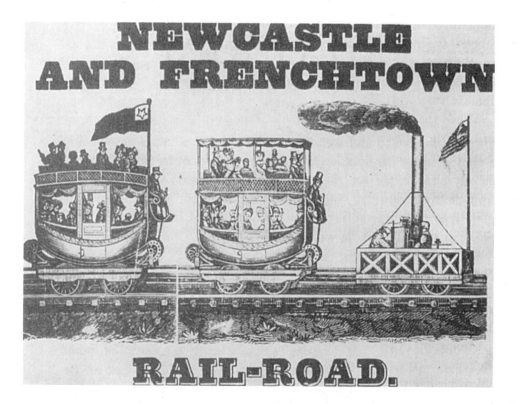

Imlay coaches (from a broadside schedule of the New-castle and Frenchtown Railroad, 1833)

were frequent, and on some of the early railroad tickets there was an agreement whereby the passenger was subject to call if needed to help replace the engine or cars on the rail. In summer weeds grew luxuriantly between the ties, and the motion of the train threw up a cloud of dust, which mixed with smoke and sparks from the locomotive and then found its way into the cars and onto the passengers. The rails on some of the early roads were simply lengths of strap iron, insecurely fastened to longitudinal wooden stringers. They were constantly coming loose, and occasionally one of them would curl up through the floor of the car and transfix a passenger. Where timber was cheap, high and rickety trestles were built in place of more substantial construction and they weaved and groaned under the weight of the trains.

The early railroads were never fenced, and, in consequence, cattle from the surrounding country used their rights of way as pastures. The light locomotives were easily derailed, and in collisions with straying stock it was not unusual for them to come off second best. To give them some advantage the cowcatcher was invented. In the hands of a daring engineer it was very effective, even if the train had to be stopped to remove fragments of beef from the locomotive.

When the first railroads were built, there were no established standards, so the gauge or distance between the rails was determined by each builder on his own. It varied on different roads from 4 feet 8½ inches, which later became standard, to the six-foot gauge of the Erie. This lack of uniformity was of small consequence so long as each railroad was an isolated unit, or even during the time, after they began to make contact, when through passengers were compelled to change trains at the end of each road. Changing trains, indeed, remained one of the standard inconveniences of travel until the sleeping-car system was perfected, and the standard-gauge railroads began to make arrangements for through passenger traffic over all connected lines. The roads built to gauges other than the standard were naturally barred from participating in these arrangements. Hence, the loss of passenger business, added to the difficulty of handling freight, finally induced them all to change to the one gauge. It is now possible to travel from coast to coast without leaving the train.

As freight and passenger traffic increased, heavier locomotives and cars were put into service and simultaneously the roadbed was improved. Inventors were busy with new forms of rail and novel switches, and as they were introduced they helped to increase the safety and comfort of travel. The present T-rail gradually came into universal use, and many of the roads were rebuilt to eliminate the sharp curves and other kinks that had been built into them originally. Crushed stone or gravel was put between and under the ties, primarily to drain the track and keep the rails in place, but also to dispose of clouds of dust in summer. In the end, prudent passengers always traveled, when possible, on ballasted roads.

By 1900, the roadbed of the first-class American railroad had taken on substantially its modern form. Heavier rails than were then made are now in use, and various signaling devices have been installed that add greatly to the safety of high-speed travel, but as far as the passenger is concerned there has been nothing added to the line that augments his immediate comfort.

2

THE
EARLY
PASSENGER
CARS

On January 7, 1830, the Baltimore & Ohio Railroad inaugurated passenger service between Mount Clare and the Carrollton Viaduct, both just outside Baltimore, with a train of four open cars, drawn by a single horse. The distance was about one and one-half miles, and a charge of nine cents was made for a round trip, or three tickets could be bought for twenty-five. While the trips during the first few months were mainly excursions for the amusement of the public, the new mode of travel instantly became popular, and on all fair days more passengers were on hand than the cars, with a capacity of about thirty passengers each, could accommodate. By the eighteenth of the month an additional car had been provided, and the five cars divided in two trains.

As the construction of the road advanced, the service was extended to more distant points, and a few closed cars were built for use in wet weather. These closed cars were little more than wooden boxes, mounted on trucks, in which the passengers sat on seats arranged around the sides. But crude as the accommodations were, there was no lack of business, and in July, 1830, the Baltimore *Gazette* reported:

Notwithstanding the great heat of the weather for the last three weeks, the amount of weekly travel on the railroad has not diminished, the average receipts being above one thousand dollars per week. In the hottest time of the hottest days the quick motion of the cars causes a current of air which renders the ride at all times agreeable. In many instances strangers passing through Baltimore, or visiting it, postpone their departure for a day and sometimes longer, to enjoy the pleasure of an additional ride on the railroad. We only repeat the general sentiment when we say, it is the most delightful of all kinds of traveling.

This was the sentiment at the time that cars were horse drawn. It changed to some extent after locomotives were introduced, but, even through the most uncomfortable periods and when complaints were the loudest, the American never lost his delight in railroad travel.

The cars making up the excursion trains and the first closed cars were built without springs, but the lack of them does not seem to have been noticed by the passengers. The railroad, at its worst, was smoother riding than the stagecoaches to which many of them were accustomed, but, as the novelty wore off, complaints apparently came in, for in the following year Jonathan Knight, the railroad's chief engineer, stated in his report that it had been "found absolutely necessary to the comfort of the passengers that carriages used for their conveyance should be mounted upon springs or some equivalent feature."

The first crude cars were soon replaced with more luxurious equipment, and the Baltimore *Gazette*, in its issue of August 14, 1830, described the most advanced model of a series of cars then going into service.

Yesterday, agreeable to notice, the splendid railroad car *Ohio* was exhibited for examination in front of the City Hotel where it remained several hours and was universally admired by a large concourse of citizens. This is the sixth car of the same class as the *Pioneer* made by that judicious and capable mechanic, Mr. Imlay, for the Baltimore & Ohio Railroad Company, and, in addition to the general advantages of beauty, comfortable arrangement and excellence of construction, which are common to the whole class, it is improved by the additional convenience of two seats the whole length of the car, with a common back, placed on and along the middle of the top, which is extended several inches in breadth over each side to increase the room, so the occupants may pass freely. The seats and back between them are cushioned and over them is an awning of canvas supported by a neat, light but sufficiently strong iron frame. The whole arrangement and finish of the top is very handsome and adds much to the general appearance as well as convenience of the car.

According to other contemporary accounts, the body of the car held twelve persons and there was room for six more, including the driver, on the outside seats at the ends of the car. The seats on the roof accommodated twelve additional passengers and, to prevent them from being thrown off by the swaying of the car, a wire netting was placed along the two sides of the top.

The trains made up of two or three of these cars were called "brigades of cars" when they were first put into service, but the use of the term was short lived. On August 27, 1830, the Baltimore & Ohio, in its advertisement in the Baltimore *Gazette*, changed to "train of cars" and continued the use of the latter term in its subsequent advertisements.

The Baltimore & Ohio cars were the first passenger cars used on an American railroad, but as other railroads came into operation similar cars were used or cars were improvised by mounting ordinary stage-coach bodies on flanged wheel trucks. On the short runs of the first few years that the railroads were in operation, the discomforts of a journey in the small cars were more than balanced by the novelty and speed of the new mode of travel, but, as the journeys lengthened, larger and better ones were needed.

Cars were built on the Imlay model that seated twenty-four passengers inside and held as many more on the roof as were able to find space, but, at best, they were uncomfortable and provided the occupants with little protection from the weather or, when drawn by a locomotive, from the sparks and smoke of the engine. The cars were divided into compartments holding six or eight people and once a passenger was in a compartment and the train in motion there was no way of getting help if needed or of communicating for other purposes with the rest of the train. A narrow board was fixed to the outside of each car on which the conductor could travel from end to end of the train, but it was a precarious journey and many conductors, in attempting it, were crushed against platforms or buildings or lost off the train.

A Harlem Railroad car of this type was noticed on Broadway by one of the staff of the *American Railroad Journal*, who described it in the issue of November 17, 1832.

> We were highly gratified on Wednesday last when we were passing up Broadway with a view of the beautiful cars of the Harlem Railroad Company. We understand they were made by Mr. Milne Parker, a coach maker of this city. They are spacious and convenient, being divided into three distinct apartments, each amply large enough for eight and can accommodate very conveniently ten persons, or twenty-four to thirty passengers inside. When we saw them there were at least, we should think, an equal number upon and hanging around the outside, the whole drawn by two fine horses abreast, at the rate of ten or twelve miles an hour. We admired their construction and believe them less liable to accident than most other we have seen, as the wheels are under the body, by which a person would be more likely, should he run against, to be thrown from than under the wheels."

Cars of this kind served their purpose after a fashion, but when the attempt was made to increase their size, troubles arose for the builders. It was found that as the body of the car was lengthened it was necessary to space the wheels farther apart to avoid excessive seesaw motion, and when this was done, great difficulty was experienced in getting around sharp curves, and there was heavy wear on the rails and wheels. A broken axle, which was a frequent occurence, was likely to cause a serious wreck, and under the best conditions derailments were among the usual features of a journey.

The Philadelphia, Germantown & Norristown Railroad produced large cars by joining two of the four-wheel coaches together and re-arranging the seats longitudinally so as to provide a passageway through the middle and an entrance at each end. Two of these, named the *Victoria* and the *President*, are reported to have been models of elegance and comfort with a bar at one end and a ladies' saloon at the other.

Four-wheel cars were in general use until 1838, and a few were still running in 1850, but they were rapidly replaced after that time by the double-truck, eight-wheel car with a center aisle that had been developed by Ross Winans for use on the Baltimore & Ohio. The Winans car was the prototype of the present day coach. One of the earliest of these cars, built in 1840 for the Tioga Railroad, survived until 1883 and was exhibited at the Chicago Railway Exposition in that year. It

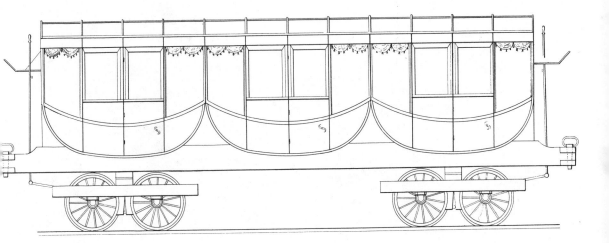

Double-truck car with three Imlay bodies (by courtesy of the Municipal Museum, Baltimore)

had a body 36 feet long, 8 feet 4 inches wide, and 6 feet 4 inches high. A single 10-inch flue in its roof, at the center of the car, provided ventilation, and two candles, one at each end of the car, furnished the illumination at night. There were no lavatories or even a water cooler, and the windows were fixed in place, the panels between them being movable. The seats, however, had iron frames similar to those in use in 1883. Such cars were built to hold from thirty to forty passengers, and most of them built at that time or later were provided with lavatories and a stove.

All of the double-truck cars had a door in each end that led out to an open platform, and the conductor as well as the passengers could travel from car to car through the train. The link and pin with which the cars were connected, however, allowed considerable motion between the ends of adjoining cars, and after a number of passengers had been crushed between cars or lost off the trains, notices were posted at all car doors warning passengers of the extreme danger of riding on the platforms or crossing to the next car. One railroad, to emphasize the danger, had a gravestone painted on the glass of each door. Another tried locking the passengers in, but after a wreck in which they were trapped in burning cars, this practice was discontinued. The early

Camden and Amboy Railroad coach, about 1836 (by
courtesy of the Pennsylvania Railroad)

American was a gregarious fellow, and in spite of all warnings he liked
to travel through the train and inquire into the business of his fellow
passengers.

He was also an inveterate tobacco-chewer with habits, when so
engaged, that were obnoxious to the lady passengers, so that some of the
best trains were shortly carrying ladies' cars, reserved for women and
any men who might be traveling with them. In these cars all the latest
comforts and conveniences were to be found, and as early as August,
1838, maid service was available. The Philadelphia, Wilmington and
Baltimore Railroad announced in its advertisement in the *Baltimore Sun*,
on the seventeenth of the month, that " cars for the accommodation of
ladies and children are provided with retiring rooms and attended by
female servants." In the ladies' car tobacco-chewing and smoking were
strictly prohibited, and notices to that effect were posted, but in the
other cars life was free and easy, and everyone made himself as comfortable as possible.

The use of a special car for women, however, seems to have been
confined chiefly to the railroads operating in the South, or running
into the South, for *Holly's Railroad Advocate* of September 20, 1856,

in commenting on the practice, said: "The New York Central commenced but soon discontinued the arrangement so much in vogue in the South, of setting the bachelors in a separate car. Probably too much space was lost, as two cars half filled had to be carried, often where one would answer if the passengers were allowed to choose their own seats. Ladies' cars are barbarisms. There is no more seclusion, nor safety against tobacco indecencies, where a lady journeys with married

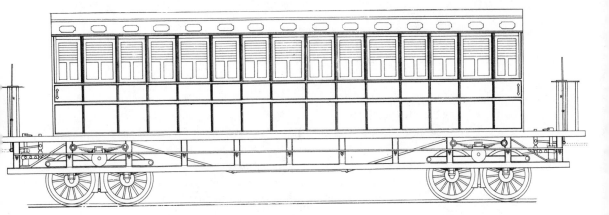

Early car with catwalks (by courtesy of the Municipal Museum, Baltimore)

gentlemen or gallants, than where she may chance to have the company of bachelors or stray benedicts. Every passenger car should have a 'saloon,' as the two by three foot closet is commonly called, but an exclusive ladies' car is usually a nuisance."

There was a feeble but constantly growing demand for better accommodations, and by the early 1840's some attention was being paid to the internal decorations and fittings of the car. The best of them were still crude affairs compared to those that came later, but every effort of the car-builders was encouraged, and the *American Railroad Journal* of June 15, 1842, joined in the general praise of six new cars, built at a cost of about $1,700 each, then going into service. It said:

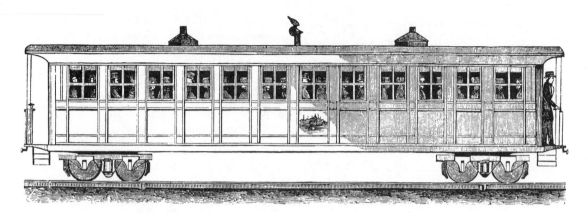

Double-truck car with center aisle, 1834 (by courtesy of the Municipal Museum, Baltimore)

We observed a few days ago a train of beautiful cars from the manufactory of Mr. Davenport (Davenport & Bridges) at Cambridge, capable of accommodating about 50 passengers each, passing on the Boston and Worcester Railroad, destined to Rochester. We were struck with the facility with which these large vehicles could be transported to such a distance, on an inland route. They probably reached Rochester on the day after they left Boston, a distance of more than 400 miles, and without being removed from the railroad track except for the purpose of being transported across the Hudson at Albany. We find the following announcement of the arrival of these cars, in the Rochester *Evening Post*:

"Yankee ingenuity is rarely more pleasantly exemplified than in the luxurious arrangement for railroad traveling of which we now have in Rochester a magnificent specimen in the splendid train of passenger cars just launched on the Auburn & Rochester Railroad. There are six cars designed to form two trains. The cars are each 28 feet long and 8 feet wide. The seats are well stuffed and admirably arranged with arms for each chair and changeable backs that will allow the passengers to change front to rear. The size of the car forms a pleasant room, handsomely painted, with floor matting; with windows secure from jarring and with curtains to shield from the blazing sun. We should have said rooms, for in four out of the six cars (the others being designed for way passengers) there is a ladies' apartment with luxurious sofas for seats and in recesses may be found a washstand and other conveniences. The arrangement for ladies we consider the greatest improvment and it will remedy some serious objections that have hitherto existed against railroad traveling on the part of families, especially where any of the members are in delicate health. The ladies may have their choice either of a sofa in their own apartment or a seat in the main saloon of the car as their health or inclination may require. The cars are hung on springs and are of such large size that they are freed from most of the jar and especially from the swinging motion so disagreeable to most railroads. The lamp of each car is so placed as to light inside and out and last but not least the breakers are so arranged so to be applied readily and with great power.

"On the whole it would be difficult to imagine any improvement that could be desired, though we dare say, these down-easters will rig up some new notion ere long that will furnish board and lodging as well as a mere passage on the railroad."

In 1843 the Erie introduced two cars, called the Diamond cars from the shape of their windows, in which the seats, upholstered in black haircloth, could be converted into couches. At that time a train could run from end to end of the Erie in three hours, and there was no night travel. The new sleeping arrangements were provided only for the convenience of passengers who wished to doze during the short day journey. The gauge of the Erie was 6 feet, and the cars were 11 feet wide. They proved to be too heavy for the railroad and were soon discontinued, and an early form of chair car was later used with more success.

There was an effort, during the 1850's, to improve on the Winans car, then becoming standardized, and some of the railroads in the East built a few cars of novel design. They were, for the most part, some form of parlor car or compartment car, more lavishly decorated than the ordinary coach. The compartment car appeared in 1853, and its arrival was announced in the *Scientific American* in August of that year:

Messers Eaton and Gilbert of Troy, N. Y., have built a beautiful car for the Hudson River Railroad which is divided into staterooms of 8 feet square. The car is 45 feet long and 9 feet 6 inches wide. Each room is calculated for a party or family and is furnished with a sofa, four chairs, a looking glass and a small center table. The panels are painted in landscapes, the ceiling hung with silk, and the floor richly carpeted. The rooms are entered by a side passage and each is well lighted and ventilated. There is a wash room in the front of the car. It is the first experiment of its kind in the United States.

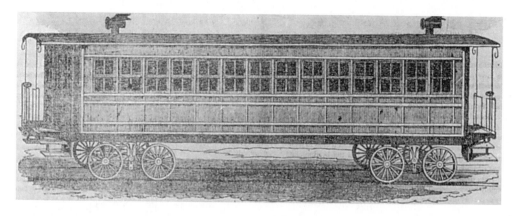

In 1856 the Baltimore & Ohio was also building cars highly decorated with landscapes and other paintings, but such decorations did not improve their riding qualities, and in the same year the newspapers were filled with complaints that there was no real progress in car design. All agreed that a car with comfortable seats was a rarity, and there was a general belief that the railroads did not install more comfortable seats, such as the reclining night chairs that had recently been invented, because they would take up more space than the roads considered the public deserved. There was also a demand that clothes hooks and racks for baggage be extended throughout the entire length of the car. The inelastic car springs, in use on most of the roads, came in for their fair share of the general criticism. Fortunately for the passengers, the jarring of the cars was as destructive to the rolling stock as it was to their comfort, and, to save the cars, the railroads toward the end of the 1850's substituted India rubber in the form of blocks. For a time it was widely used, but the rubber then available rapidly lost its resiliency, becoming rigid or frozen, and by 1865 it was going out of favor, to return in recent years.

Between 1850 and 1860 a few cars were built that seated as many as seventy-two passengers, for it was thought that it added to a railroad's prestige to operate large cars, but the general rule was to build them to seat sixty people. Some of the large cars were built at the Piedmont

Railroad car, 1845 (from the *Scientific American,* August, 1845)

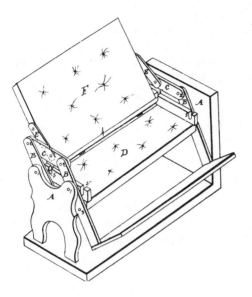

C. P. Bailey car seat (patented by C. P. Bailey, October 10, 1854, No. 11772)

shops of the Erie, and their salient features were noted in Colburn's *Railroad Advocate* of July 19, 1856:

These cars are not equaled in size, accommodation, or elegance of finish by any other public railroad conveyance in the world. Whatever may be the opinion as to the policy of running so heavy cars, universal admiration must be yielded to their comfort and luxurious finish.

The body of the car is 60 feet 3 inches long, outside, and 10 feet 9 inches wide. The posts are 7 feet high and the height of the car at the center is about 11 inches greater than that of any other car now on the road. There are 20 windows on each side of the car, with a single plate of double thick French plate glass, 17 by 21 inches, in each. There are two windows also in each end. The car seats 74 passengers, including two in the saloon.

The outside finish of the cars is singular and neat. There are three plain vertical panels under each window and one long panel, reaching from the sills to the cap, between every two windows.

The seats, throughout, are C. P. Bailey's patented reclining, day or night seats. They are very large and easy and splendidly upholstered, the covering being a rich velvet plush, costing five dollars a yard. Over one hundred yards of plush were used.

The cars are ventilated on Foote & Hayes' patented plan, which is the most comfortable means of purifying, cooling and equalizing the temperature of the air in passenger cars. The side " pedestals," as they are called, in which the ventilating water fountains play, are elegantly finished off and a large plate glass in each gives a view of the cooling spray when the car is running. Through these pedestals the air is conducted from the air cap, on the roof, to the registers in the floor. There are four pivot seats, on each corner of each pedestal, moulded and upholstered in a most luxurious style. They are decidedly a new feature in passenger cars, although a very few are already in use in one or two other new cars on the same road.

The head-lining is an expensive and rich pattern, although not quite in good taste with the rest. In some of the other cars a new pattern will, perhaps, be adopted. The gilt cornice around the inside is 4 inches deep and very rich. The entire weight of these cars, empty, is not far from 18 tons.

Shortly after the Erie cars were put into service, the convertible sleeping car, built and operated by sleeping car companies, put in an appearance and from then on the great improvements in car design and fittings were to be found in the cars of these companies. The railroads, for the most part, confined themselves to the standardized pattern. Many of the comforts and conveniences of the sleeping cars were introduced into the coaches, but there was a considerable lag, and the coaches did not keep pace with the more luxurious equipment. The lag, to a large extent, was due to the financial inability of the railroads to scrap still serviceable rolling stock, but the dislike of the general public for anything unfamiliar entered into it. Many of the railroads have, at various times, tried out new ideas in coach design only to find that the public preferred the old.

3

SERVICE

AND

FITTINGS

Although early railroad journeys were short, many of the passengers had occasion to carry baggage or other impedimenta with them on their travels and, as there was little room in the cars to store it, the great bulk of it was carried on the tops of the cars. This method of conveying baggage was the cause of much delay to the trains as well as of damage to the cars, and it called for considerable labor by the train's crew. A few years' experience showed the railroads the need for separate cars for baggage, and when the Camden and Amboy hauled its first train with a locomotive, there was a baggage car attached. An account of the trip appeared in *Niles' Register* of September 28, 1833:

> On Monday of last week the cars of the Camden and Amboy Railroad were started for the first time with a locomotive engine. From Amboy to Bordentown the cars went over finely and back as far as Heightstown. There an unlucky hog got under the traveler of the locomotive and, in endeavoring to run out between the fore and hind wheels, was instantly decapitated. The locomotive was thrown off and plunged with its head into the gutter, and the baggage car, which followed immediately after, was also thrown off. But the passengers remained undisturbed except that one gentleman, in the fright, turned a summerset out of the window.

Shortly thereafter the Baltimore & Ohio put baggage cars into service.

The passengers on all railroads, however, had to sort out and look after their own baggage, for the railroads assumed no responsibility for either loss or damage and, to emphasize the fact, caused notices reading, "All Baggage at the Owner's Risk," or signs similarly worded, to be posted in all railroad stations. For a time such signs were considered sufficient notice, and in the face of them the great majority of people who suffered a loss were unwilling to start legal proceedings against a powerful railroad corporation, but eventually a few of the more hardy took their cases to court and were uniformly successful. The courts took the attitude that if the railroads were not held responsible, there was nothing to prevent them from engaging thieves to loot the passengers' baggage and sharing in the spoils.

By 1838 the status of the railroads as common carriers, with the accompanying liabilities, was firmly established, and they set about devising a system for handling the baggage that would assure that at least a reasonable portion of it arrived at its proper station. Marking each piece with chalk to show its destination was first tried, but the chalk marks were easily erased or blurred, and the method was otherwise unsatisfactory. It was followed by the use of duplicate brass checks, one of which was fastened to the baggage and the other held by the passenger as a receipt until he received his baggage at the end of his journey. Barring accident, this system worked, and the passenger usually recovered his baggage, but too often, if the early reports are to be believed, he only recovered that fragment to which the check was attached, the balance of it being scattered over the baggage-car floor or the station platform. The general belief that the functionaries who handled the baggage took a fiendish delight in destroying it soon earned for them the title of baggage-smashers, which is traced by the *Dictionary of American English* to 1856 and is probably older, and it stayed with them for many years. The duplicate-check system has survived to the present day, but the brass checks have long since disappeared, and cardboard checks are now used in place of them.

As the car developed into the form that was to survive for years, the attention of the car-builders was directed more and more to the internal fittings, including illumination. In the early days travel by night was a dark and gloomy business. The cars were lighted by candles, one at each end, and in the dim light reading and other pastimes were

impossible. For years after oil lamps were in general use for home
illumination, most of the railroads continued using candles, for there
was less danger of fire from them than from oil. As cars of greater
length were built, however, illuminating them by candles became more
difficult and expensive, and by 1870 the great majority of cars in service
were equipped with kerosene lamps.

These lamps gave a brighter light than candles, but they flickered and
smoked in every draft, and their fumes saturated the car. Improvements
were made in the burners, but at best the light was dim, and various
systems were therefore tried using compressed coal gas, first used in a
car on the Galena and Chicago Railroad between Chicago and Fulton
on December 27, 1856, gasoline vapors generated by the Frost car-
buretor, or gas distilled from crude petroleum by the Pintsch method.
Of these, the brilliant Pintsch was the best. It had practically replaced
all the others when electric lighting was perfected and came into general
use.

The early car seat built to accommodate two passengers was a hard
and uncomfortable piece of furniture, and even after its hardness had
been relieved by the use of upholstery, its back was still built only
to the height of an ordinary chair and thus afforded no support for the

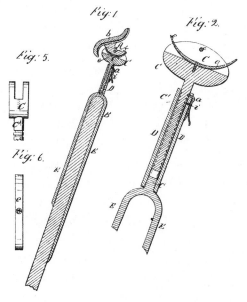

Early headrest (patented by W. M. McCauley,
September 1, 1857, No. 18122)

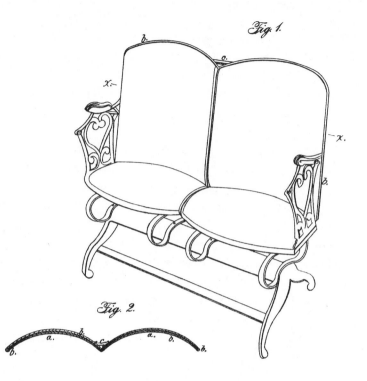

Individual car seat (patented by T. E. Warren, July, 30, 1850, No. 7539)

passenger's head. Peddlers did a thriving business at the railroad stations selling portable headrests, which were devices made of steel, attachable to the low backs of the seats and adjustable to fit the passenger's head. There was no lack of suggestions for better seats, and as early as 1850 a type of individual seat was patented. This was followed in 1852 by a reclining seat and by a number of others within the next few years, but cars with really comfortable seats did not come into general use until 1871. Those in the first sleeping cars had the same low backs, and it was not until the 1870's that a model was made with a back that reached the passenger's shoulders. The 1880's were well advanced before backs were built high enough to support the passenger's head.

In the first days of the railroad, because of the greater available speed, passengers were satisfied to travel only by day, but as greater distances were covered in continuous journeys, there was a demand for trains

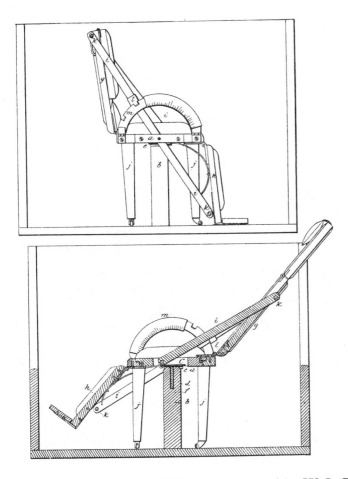

Reclining seat (patented by W. L. Bass, July 20, 1852, No. 9128)

that ran through the night. Sitting all day on the hard, stiff seats was uncomfortable enough, but a night journey on the same seats in a dark, stuffy car produced discomforts that shook the hardiest passenger. Anything was better than the seats then in use, and in 1836 the Cumberland Valley Railroad put a crude form of sleeping car or bunk car into service. The other railroads followed, and in a short time sleeping cars of one sort or another were in use on most of the roads that ran trains at night. They were for male passengers exclusively, and only for those who were not particularly squeamish, but as the West was settled and night journeys became a commonplace of travel, a reasonably comfortable sleeping car became a necessity, and by 1860 over twenty types had been patented, some of which were put into actual service.

These cars solved, to a large extent, the problem of travel by night, but travel by day was still far from ideal. When the railroads had been built to such distances that it was possible to make a continuous journey of more than a few hours, some means had to be found of feeding the passengers. Some of them carried their food with them, but others preferred to eat along the road, and these took advantage of the frequent stops to get out and forage.

Eatinghouses quickly sprang up at junction points, and as traffic increased, dining stations or refreshment saloons, as they were called, were established by the railroads themselves at the towns along the line. A few were excellent and their meals became famous, but most of them were second rate, and in a number the food was inedible. The railroads made constant efforts to improve the poor ones, but many of them were let as concessions, and the roads had little control over them. The system worked fairly well, but it had features that inconvenienced the railroads as well as the passengers.

All through trains were delayed as much as an hour a day to allow time for meals to be eaten, which took from ten to twenty minutes for each meal. In that limited time there was a wild scramble among the passengers to get down at least part of a meal before the train pulled out. In winter or in stormy weather many people were reluctant to leave the train, and the old and infirm were barred from eating in such places at any time.

The meals were spaced to suit the schedule, and the passengers might get all three meals within a few hours on one section of the road and fast for long periods between meals on another. If the train was delayed, they would be without food for hours except for such provender as the news butcher brought round. Each eating place usually had its specialty, which was served every day. After the telegraph came into use, it was the custom of the conductor to go through the train some time before it was due at a dining station and ask all passengers who intended to eat there to signify the fact. He would then telegraph ahead, so that the proper number of meals could be prepared. Where chicken was the house dish, this was the signal to start killing, and cases are reported by imaginative travelers of chickens still kicking when brought to the table. That the food was purposely served too hot to be eaten in the limited time, and was re-served to those on the train following, also seems to have been a popular belief.

On June 10, 1857, the *New York Times* summed up the shortcomings of the refreshment saloons, and the same might have been as truthfully said about them at any time thereafter:

If there is any word in the English language more shamefully misused than another, it is the word refreshment, as applied to the hurry scurry of eating and drinking at railroad stations. The dreary places in which the painful and unhealthy performances take place are called Refreshment Saloons, but there could not be a more inappropriate designation for such abominations of desolation. Directors of railroads appear to have an idea that travelers are destitute of stomach; that eating and drinking are not at all necessary to human beings bound on long journeys, and that nothing more is required than to put them through their misery in as brief a time as possible. It is expected that three or four hundred men, women and children, some of whom must, of necessity, be feeble folk and unaccustomed to roughing it, and all of whom have been used to the decencies and comforts of orderly homes, can be whirled half a day over a dusty road, with hot cinders flying in their faces; and then, when they approach a station dying with weariness, hunger and thirst, longing for an opportunity to bathe their faces at least before partaking of their much needed refreshments, that they shall rush out helter-skelter into a dismal, long room and dispatch a supper, breakfast or dinner in fifteen minutes. The consequences of such savage and unnatural feeding are not reported by telegraph as railroad disasters; but if a faithful account were taken of them we are afraid they would be found much more serious than any that are caused by the smashing of cars, or the breaking of bridges. The traveler who has been riding all night in a dusty and crowded car, unable to sleep, and half suffocated with smoke and foul air, will be suddenly roused from his half lethargic condition by hearing the scream of the steam whistle, which tells of the near approach to a station; but before the train stops, the door of the car opens, and the conductor shouts at the top of his voice, " Pogramville—fifteen minutes for breakfast! "

Here is a prospect for a weary and hungry traveler to whom fifteen minutes would be brief time enough for ablutions. But washing is out of the question, even if all the conveniences were at hand, and he rushes into the "saloon" where he is offered a choice of fried ham and eggs, or tough beefsteak soaked in bad butter, tea and coffee, stale bread; the inevitable custard pie and pound cake, are also at his service; but half the fifteen minutes allowed for breakfast having been lost while waiting for a turn at one of the two washbasins, the bewildered traveler makes a hasty grab at whatever comes within his reach, and hurries back to his seat, to discover before he reaches the end of his journey, that he has laid the foundation for a fit of dyspepsia, which may lead to a disease of the lungs or a fever.

A company that expends thirty millions of dollars in building and equipping a road, ought not to begrudge a few hundred dollars in furnishing a suitable place for travelers to refresh themselves at, nor deny them the necessary time to do it in. Refreshment saloons ought to be under the charge of the railroad company, for passengers ought not to be put at the mercy of grasping and ignorant men, who are regardless of everything but their own profit. There are very few roads in the whole country on which there is a station where a comfortable meal can be obtained, or where the necessary accommodations are to be found which passengers require when they stop. The Erie road has the most comfortable and spacious cars of any railroad in the country, and we have no doubt that it would be a great accession of travel if there were decent station-houses on the line for the refreshment of passengers, and the arrangement of the time-tables were such that they could be enjoyed. As our great lines of railroad are laid through wild and half cultivated regions, where the common refinements of City life are not to be looked for, the railroad managers should themselves make the necessary provision for the refreshment of passengers which they have a right to expect. As affairs are now arranged, a few days of railroad traveling are sure to end in a fit of sickness to all excepting those who have hearty constitutions, and are accustomed to the very roughest and toughest manner of living.

Dining cars had been proposed as early as 1838 and at intervals thereafter, and in 1863 two restaurant cars were put into service on the Philadelphia, Wilmington and Baltimore Railroad and operated for several years. These were ordinary day coaches with cross partitions at their centers. Half of the car was used for a smoker, and in the other half, from which the seats had been removed, an eating bar, with a steam box, was installed. The food was cooked at the terminals and carried in the steam box, and the bar was probably patronized by men only. It was not until 1867 that the first diner was put into service. In that year George M. Pullman introduced his first so-called hotel

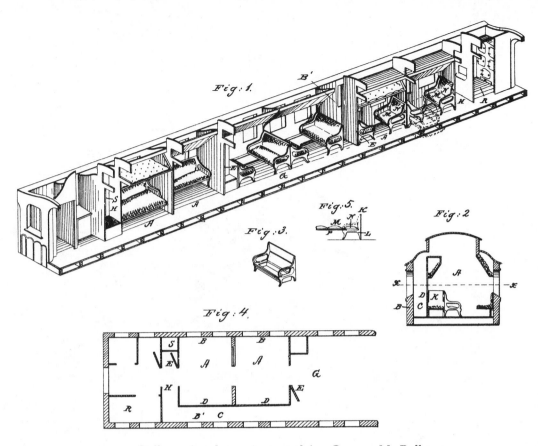

Pullman hotel car (patented by George M. Pullman, April 27, 1869, No. 89538)

car on the Great Western Railroad of Canada. This was a sleeper with a small kitchen in one end, and the meals were served on tables that were set up, when needed, between the seats. There was an ample supply of elegant crockery and table linen, and the passengers were given their choice of a number of dishes prepared by a professional cook. These comforts, however, were reserved for the occupants of the car. The advantage of allowing the other passengers to eat aboard were apparent to everyone, and in 1868 Pullman placed the first dining car open to all passengers in service on the Chicago & Alton.

In these first diners the kitchen was placed in the center, in order, as Pullman stated in his patent papers of April 27, 1869, " that in whatever direction the car may be traveling at least half of it will be in advance

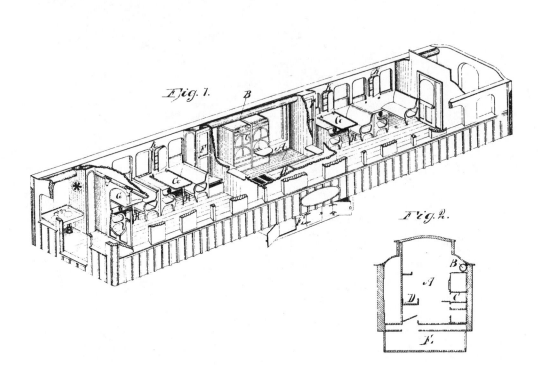

First Pullman dining car (patented by George M. Pullman, April 27, 1869, No. 89537)

of the kitchen, the odors of which are borne by the draught toward the rear." The first car, named the *Delmonico*, was quickly followed by others, and the dining stations gradually disappeared. Some of them, however, survived until after the turn of the century, especially in the South and West. The Pullman Company operated dining cars for a number of years, but, the business not proving profitable, it finally withdrew, and since that time they have been operated by the various railroads, also usually at a loss.

The introduction of the diner was the first step toward converting

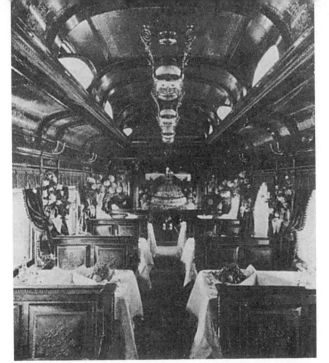

Interior of the dining car *Waldorf*, attached to the Baltimore & Ohio's *Royal Limited*, 1890 (by courtesy of the Baltimore & Ohio Railroad)

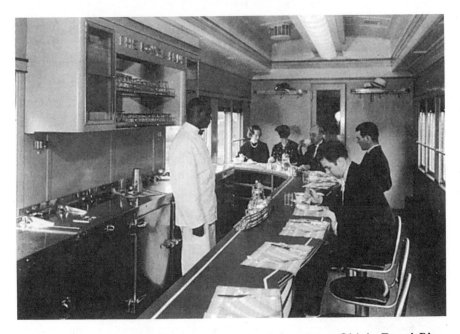

Lunch counter on the Baltimore & Ohio's *Royal Blue* (by courtesy of the Baltimore & Ohio Railroad)

Dining at sixty miles an hour (about 1880) (by courtesy of the Baltimore & Ohio Railroad)

the entire train into one unit. Previous to that time there was no necessity for a passenger to move from one car to another while the train was in motion, but to reach the diner he had to travel through the train and cross the dangerous platforms. This intercar traffic became heavier when chaircars, first used in 1875 by the larger railroads, and various other varieties of so-called palace cars were attached to the train, and a number of methods were proposed for bridging the space between the cars or for enclosing the platforms so that they could be crossed in safety and comfort. The greatest hazard faced by a passenger crossing from car to car was not due so much to the space between the cars as to the violent swaying of the platforms when the train was running at high speed, and no effective method was devised for checking this motion until Henry Howard Sessions introduced his vertical end frame, or friction plates, in 1887. Sessions, who was superintendent of the Pullman Company at the time, developed his invention in the Pullman plant and received his patent on November 15 of the same year. The vertical end frame was designed not only to reduce the violent motions of the platforms, but also, and chiefly, to act as a buffer between the cars and

Combination smoking and baggage car with open platforms (by courtesy of the Municipal Museum, Baltimore)

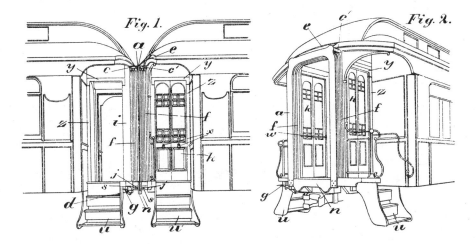

Vertical end frame (patented by H. H. Sessions, November 15, 1887, No. 373098)

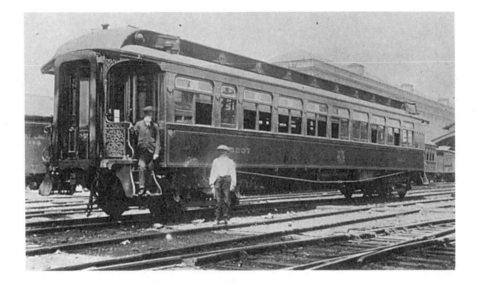

Original form of the vestibule (by courtesy of the Municipal Museum, Baltimore)

cushion the sudden jerk and the racking of the cars when the train was started or brought to a stop. It was adaptable for use on cars with open platforms as well as on those with closed, and Sessions disclaimed the vestibule as a part of his invention.

The first vestibules used in connection with the vertical end frame were only as wide as the car door and did not, as at present, enclose the entire platform. But with their use a safe passage was assured between the cars, and they ended the dangerous practice of some passengers boarding and leaving the train while it was in motion. These vestibules came into general use on all Pullmans within a few years after they were first introduced on the Pennsylvania in 1887. With their coming, the standard American train took on its modern form. It was no longer a series of cars coupled together, but had become in effect one continuous car that extended from end to end of the train.

Early vestibule car (by courtesy of the Baltimore &
Ohio Railroad)

4

THE

METAL

CAR

The vestibule train, with all the luxurious cars that were a part of it, seemed, at the time it was introduced, to be the height of comfort. The cars making up the train were comfortable enough, although their ventilation was defective and dust and smoke still came aboard, but, as they were built largely of wood, they were no safer in case of accident than the ones that had preceded them. The passenger still ran the risk, as before, of ending his journey by being pulverized or cre-

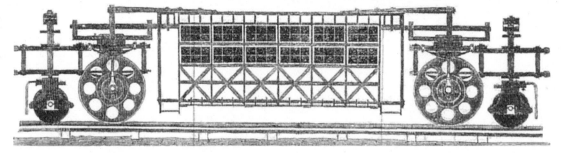

Underslung car (from the *Scientific American*, March 19, 1846)

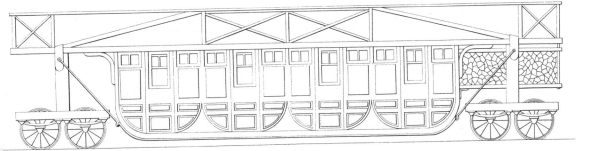

Underslung car with four Imlay-type bodies (courtesy
of the Municipal Museum, Baltimore)

mated. To minimize the danger from wrecks, cars built partly or
entirely of metal had been suggested at different times, and a particularly bad accident usually produced a new crop of ideas.

As far back as 1846 H. L. Lewis offered a car constructed entirely
of wrought iron that he claimed was lighter but of greater strength
than the wooden cars then in use and had the additional advantage of
being cheaper to build and less expensive to maintain. The maintenance on a wooden car, he stated, in three years amount to the original
cost of the car. To keep the center of gravity of the car body low
and provide room for the large wheels, he moved the frame from its
usual position under the body of the car and placed it above, with the
car body suspended from it. The underslung principle was not new
with him, for it had been suggested some time before. The car was
intended for use at high speed, and the wheels carrying the load were
made large to reduce friction in the bearings. The only purpose of the
small wheels was to keep the car on the track. So far as is known,
Lewis' car was never built; but the idea of an underslung car has
cropped up from time to time since.

In 1847 the Albany and Buffalo covered its mail cars with tin to
protect them from sparks, and in 1851 T. E. Warren, of Troy, designed
a very ornate wrought-iron car, which he patented on October 18, 1853
(No. 10142). Warren's principal claims were for the structural fea-

Warren's wrought-iron car (from the *Scientific American*, August, 1851)

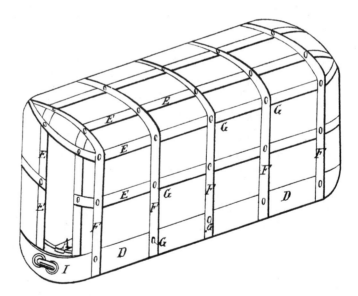

Steel frame of the LaMothe car (patented by Bernard J. LaMothe, April 4, 1854, No. 10721)

tures of the sides of his car. These were constructed of thin sheets of iron, stiffened and strengthened by hollow columns formed of sheet iron, which made the sides and were, in effect, plate girders. The body of the car was supported by the sides, and the floor and roof were rigidly connected to them with through bolts.

The LaMothe car, patented by Dr. B. J. LaMothe in 1854, was developed in Patterson, New Jersey, with funds provided by E. W. Sargent, a Patterson merchant. The metal frame of LaMothe's car, which was the principal part of his invention, was constructed, in the form of a cage, of elastic steel bars that were fastened at their intersections with rivets or screws. The great advantage claimed for the car, over the ordinary wooden car, was its high resistance to telescoping and breaking up in case of an accident. To protect the occupants further, the car was lined throughout with a soft and yielding material. As originally designed it had a floor of the usual wooden construction, and LaMothe probably intended to cover the exterior with the same material. He did not claim, in his patent papers, that the car was fireproof.

Several railroads combined to experiment with the car, among them

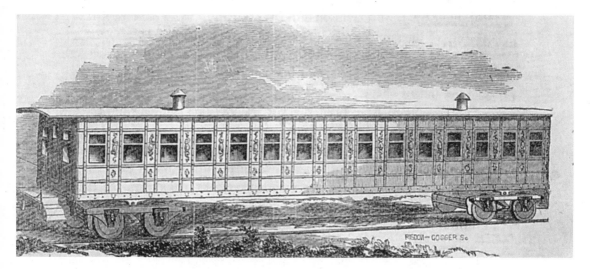

LaMothe car (from the *American Railroad Journal*, January, 1856)

the Boston and Worcester and the New York & Erie, and one was built in 1859. It was forty-six feet long, with thirty seats, and did not differ materially in appearance from the ordinary wooden cars of the same class, although no wood was used in its construction. The interior was lined with several layers of thick pasteboard for insulation, and the pasteboard was covered with heavy cushions. It was operated on the New York & Erie for about six months and then sent to Boston for trial on the Boston and Worcester in the early part of 1860. Three more LaMothe cars are reported to have been built, but nothing more is known about them.

In November, 1860, a trial run was made on the Pittsburgh, Fort Wayne & Chicago Railroad with an iron car that was self-propelled. It weighed seventeen tons and had the capacity of two ordinary coaches. Such propelled cars—that is, with a boiler and engine in one end—were coming into use at the time. There was such a car, the *Novelty*, in operation on the Western Division of the Pennsylvania Central Railroad in the same year, and in 1861 a number of the same type were built in Philadelphia, by Grice and Long, for use on a southern road, but these cars and the *Novelty* were built of wood.

In 1862 the Eastern Railroad was operating a baggage car made of iron plates, and in June, 1863, the New York Central sent out an iron car, built by J. M. Davidson & Son at Albany, on an experimental run. In July of the same year it was loaded with notables and sent to Niagara Falls, but it does not seem to have been a success. It was returned to Rochester empty, full of dents and showing signs of having been badly twisted out of shape.

This seems to have been the last use of such equipment for many years. With the abundant timber then available, wooden cars were far cheaper to build than metal cars, and there was also the fear that in a wreck, unless the entire train was made up of metal cars, those so built would plow through the wooden coaches making up the balance of the train and kill or maim everyone in them. However, the interest in metal cars continued, and in the course of the next three decades a number of ideas were worked out, among them that of making pressed steel sections, which proved to be of great value when the all-metal car eventually arrived.

Following the extensive timber cutting of the 1870's and 1880's, the car-builders found themselves facing a diminishing timber supply at the same time that there was a demand for larger and stronger cars. The cars by then had reached such sizes and weights that it was practically impossible to get timber of the required dimensions, and, in place of the solid timber previously used, various types of wooden trusses, borrowed from the bridge-builders, were framed into the car to support the body. Such construction increased the weight without a corresponding increase in strength, and by the end of the century steel was being substituted for wood in those parts of the car where great strength was required. The all-metal car followed as a matter of course, and in 1906 several of the railroads had it in service. In 1907 the first all-metal Pullman sleeper appeared, and by 1910 it was in general use.

The first steel cars of the latter period squeaked and groaned like a ship at sea, and the efforts to imitate the elaborate finish of the wooden coaches, by painting the steel plates to simulate mahogany and parquetry, were not overly successful, but better construction eliminated the noises, and eventually a more suitable system of decoration was used on the interiors.

∽ 5 ∽

VENTILATION
AND
HEATING

Present-day ventilating devices, especially those for use in winter, would have been considered highly dangerous by most of the passengers who rode the railroads in the early days, and the car-builders, in keeping with the times, gave little attention to the airing of their cars. In hot weather it was the custom of the male passengers to open the windows and rest both feet on the window sill, and a train with a pair of feet projecting out of each window was not an unusual sight. In winter the stove was kept at a red heat, and since the cars had no effective ventilators, the only fresh air that entered came in a blast when the door was opened or leaked in through the floor and chilled the passengers' feet. The fumes from the hot and rancid animal fats used to lubricate the axles entered with the air.

Besides the lack of controlled ventilation there was always the presence of smoke and, in dry weather, dust, often mixed with sparks from the locomotive. In summer, when the windows were open, or in winter, when the door was open, clouds of the mixture entered and were the cause of more complaints from the passengers than all their other discomforts together.

It was the custom, in the first few years of the railroads, for the passengers to dress themselves in their best when starting on a journey by rail, but they soon found that the dust and sparks made a sorry wreck of their finery, and by the middle 1840's more rugged clothes were being worn. Later, when the dust clouds were at their greatest, it became the fashion to wear a " duster," a long coat made of linen or other light material, over the ordinary clothes, and an occasional passenger so equipped was still to be met within relatively recent years.

Various schemes were proposed to obviate the smoke and spark nuisance, among them that of extending the smokestack of the locomotive back over the cars to the rear of the train. Passing the smoke through jets of water to quench the sparks was suggested, but there were objections to all such ideas, and most locomotives were eventually equipped with some form of spark-arrester, built into their smokestacks.

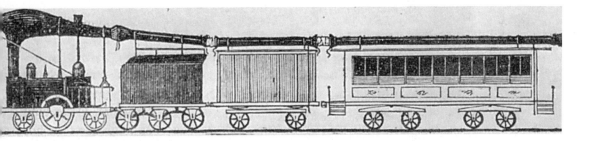

Towsend's horizontal smoke pipe (from the *Scientific American*, April 24, 1847)

Such spark-arresters were widely used after the late 1830's, and the gigantic, conical-shaped smokestacks that housed them became a familiar feature of the wood-burning locomotive. As coal replaced wood as fuel there was a resulting reduction in the smoke and cinders, but the nuisance remained in part to annoy the passengers in summer until the modern system of air conditioning was perfected.

As speeds increased, during the 1850's, there was a vast increase in the clouds of dust thrown up by the trains, and the railroads were beset on all sides with complaints. Passenger business fell off, and the railroads were in a receptive mood for schemes for keeping dust and smoke out of the cars. Many were proposed, but most of them were impracticable and few of them were ever put to use. They consisted for the most part of some arrangement of screens, blinds, wind wheels,

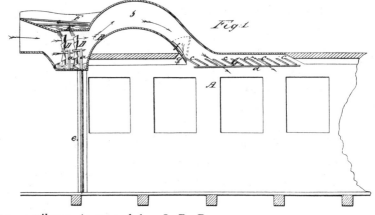

Air-cleaning ventilator (patented by J. B. Bausman, April 9, 1861, No. 31943)

or shutters projecting from the outside of the car at various places, often at the windows. The purpose of the projections was to deflect the currents of air set up by the motion of the train and, by the partial vacuum thus formed, cause an outward flow of air from the car through the openings provided. The air to replace it was admitted through some form of ventilator, usually placed on top of the car, and baffles or small water tanks were incorporated in its construction to clean the air before it entered the car. Some of the inventors dispensed with the deflectors and depended on a ventilator of special design to admit the air to the car and clean it during its passage.

The apparatus patented by H. M. Paine on January 6, 1852, and used on the New York and New Haven Railroad was typical of many such devices, except that it hinged the car windows and utilized them for deflecting the air currents. V. P. Corbett, who patented a ventilator on November 13, 1855, depended on baffles built into the ventilator to clean the incoming air and allowed it to find its way out of the car through the cracks and crevices in the car body. He claimed in his patent papers that "this ventilator has been tried upon some of the cars of the main railroads and found to answer the purpose admirably," but he did not name the railroads on which it was used.

In 1855 some of the trains of the Hartford & New Haven Railroad were equipped with a device patented by E. C. Salisbury on July 31,

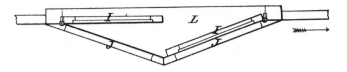

Ventilating window (patented by H. M. Paine, January 6, 1852, No. 8645)

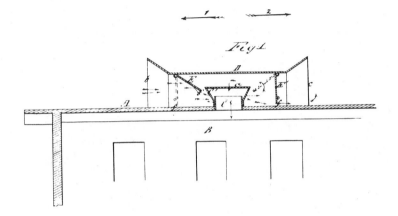

Car-ventilator (patented by V. P. Corbett, November 13, 1855, No. 13779)

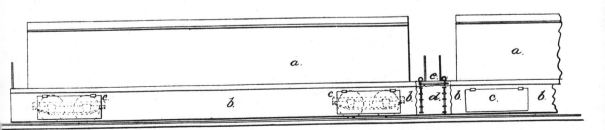

Dust tunnel (patented by Elam C. Salisbury, July 31, 1855, No. 13364)

1855, and called, in his patent papers, a ventilator, though it was actually a dust-collector. It consisted of curtains, which could be made of wood, metal, canvas, or any other suitable material, built along the sides of the car and extending outside the trucks to within a short distance of the rails. The curtains of adjoining cars were connected at the platforms so as to form a continuous tunnel under the train in which the dust thrown up from the roadbed was confined until it was expelled from the rear of the last car. In addition to collecting the dust, the curtains deadened the noise of the train, so that it was possible to carry on an ordinary conversation in the cars. They also prevented passengers from falling under the train when boarding or leaving.

Charles Atwood, who patented his improvements in ventilating cars on July 10, 1855, had somewhat the same idea as Salisbury, except that he made a continuous tunnel of the cars themselves and admitted clean air to them by way of air ducts leading to the tender of the locomotive. To prevent leakage of air out of the cars or dust into them at the platforms, he adopted the vestibule proposed by Charles Waterbury in 1852 for making travel across the platforms safe, and he improved it by adding vertical end frames and flexible connections.

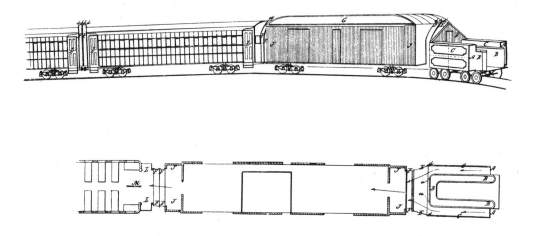

Air tunnel (patented by Charles Atwood, July 10, 1855, No. 13204)

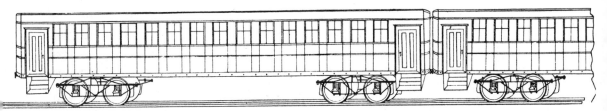

Early vestibule (patented by Charles Waterbury, June 29, 1852, No. 9084)

But such devices gave little relief, for most of the dust and cinders escaped through them and came aboard the cars. About the same time, another group of inventors were developing ventilating systems along more modern lines. All in this group used an air-washer of some sort, with an anticipated capacity sufficient to remove all the dust and cinders from the incoming air, and arranged the air ducts and other parts around it. Some provided refrigeration to cool the air in summer, and most of them included a stove, often of novel design, to warm the washed air in winter. One of them, E. B. Forbough, taking into account the suffocating and usually fetid atmosphere in the cars in winter, went a step further and claimed in his patent papers, February 21, 1860 (No. 27212), that "a cloth or sponge, saturated with odoriferous extracts and hung in the room occupied by the stove will add very much to the salubrity and sweetness of the air as it passes into the car."

There was considerable ingenuity shown in the design of the air-washers and a number of methods were used for bringing the air into contact with the water. For the most part the washing was done either with water jets, by passing the air over the surface of water, or by forcing it through wetted screens or through water. When water jets were used, or the air was merely passed over water, it was admitted to the washer through a ventilator or a bonnet projecting from the exterior of the car, and the volume of air flowing through the system was dependent on the amount forced into the ventilators or bonnet by the forward motion of the train. Under the most favorable conditions the pressure that could be created in this way was not sufficient to force air through wetted screens or water, so whenever either of these methods was used for washing, an air pump or a blower, driven off an axle of the car, was provided to furnish the necessary pressure. However the air-washers operated, none of them would function until the train was in motion, and if there was a strong tail wind, those depending entirely on the forward motion of the train for their air supply probably did not function too well then.

The use of ice for cooling the air in summer was suggested as early as 1852 by a Daniel Flynn, and the idea was adopted by all those following him who included refrigeration in their ventilating systems. Most of these appliances were operated on an open system, that is, the air after circulating in the car was allowed to escape through vents or other openings. Refrigeration in such cases was an optional benefit, as the temperature in the car could not rise above the temperature of the outside air while the train was in motion. But in some trains a closed system was used, and a large part of the air that entered the car was recovered and recirculated. In these, refrigeration of some kind was necessary, for without it the air in the car would become heated to an insufferable degree. A ventilating and cooling apparatus of this type was patented by Job R. Barry on May 15, 1855.

In one end of a tank, suspended from the floor of the car, Barry placed an icebox and in the other end two or more paddle wheels made of wire gauze or cloth and driven off an axle of the car. The wheels were partly submerged in water from the melted ice and as they revolved air was forced through them by a blower. The air was pre-cooled and cleaned in its passage through the paddle wheels and then passed through the icebox and into the car. After circulating in the car, a small part, one-tenth, was allowed to escape through vents and

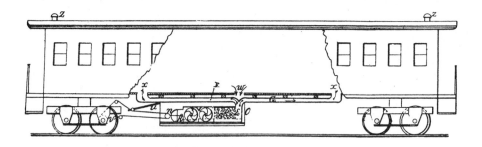

Barry's recirculating system (patented by Job R. Barry, May 15, 1855, No. 12851)

openings in the body; the balance was recovered, mixed with outside air, and recirculated through the system. Barry claimed a temperature of about fifty degrees for the air entering the car and stated that "its temperature may be reduced to as low a degree as comfort can require."

There is no account of ice alone being used for cooling cars during these early years, and if it was attempted, it was probably discovered, as it was many years later, that the amount required was prohibitive and that supplying the cars was an insoluble problem. In lieu of ice, the water used for washing the air was usually depended on to cool it, and if the temperature was not greatly reduced thereby, the freshness imparted to the air by the washing seems to have greatly pleased the passengers.

A few of these appliances got past the experimental stage and were installed by George F. Foote and described in his patent papers as a

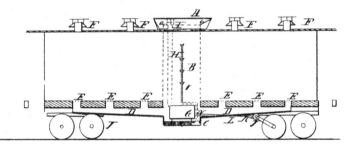

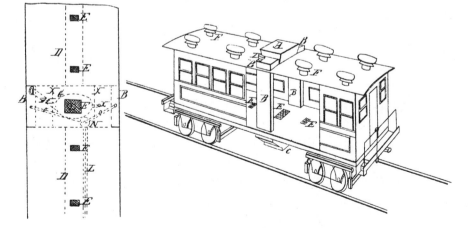

Foote & Hayes air-washer (patented by George F. Foote, July 11, 1854, No. 11268)

"new and improved mode of ventilating and heating railroad cars and excluding the dust therefrom." The use of water jets was not original with Foote, for they had been used for condensing the acid fumes from smelters and had also been proposed for quenching the sparks in the smoke from locomotives. His claims were for the novel design of the nozzles he used and for other parts of the equipment, as well as for the general arrangement.

The air supply for Foote's washer entered through a bonnet (A) erected on the roof of the car at its center. The openings in the bonnet were covered with fine mesh to deflect sparks and cinders and to condense the smoke, on the principle of the Davey safety lamp. On each side of the car there was a vertical duct or "pedestal" (B) through which the air traveled downward from the bonnet and in which the water jets (H) played. Water for the jets was supplied by a pump (J) driven by a belt off an axle of the car, and a supply of water was carried in a tank (C) suspended from the floor. After being washed, the air passed to a duct (D) under the floor, running lengthwise along the car and then to the passengers through openings (E) in the duct. The foul air was discharged outside the car. A stove (G), placed on the water tank and fed through a trap door in the car floor, warmed the air in winter.

Foote received his patent on July 11, 1854, and in August of the same year he assigned to the Michigan Southern and the Northern Indiana railroad companies his rights and interests in any of his ventilating systems that might be used on their roads. On March 21, 1855, he formed a partnership with Joel N. Hayes under the firm name of Foote & Hayes, and on April 1 of the following year he assigned a half interest in his patent to Hayes.

Trouble quickly developed on the Michigan Southern. The belt driving the water pump constantly ran off the pulley, and after a short trial the washer was abandoned for that reason. But this was premature, for the defect was subsequently corrected by the substitution of a friction drive suggested by Calvin A. Smith, master car-builder in the Piedmont shop of the Erie.

Foote & Hayes equipment was installed in the large seventy-two-passenger cars built by the Erie in 1856, and it was in use on that road, and on one of the railroads connecting Cleveland and Cincinnati, in

1857. What success it had on the Northern Indiana does not appear in the record, and except for the short trial on the Michigan Central, it is not known to have been used on any other railroad.

During the same period Henry Jones Ruttan was developing and promoting his ventilating system. Ruttan, a citizen of Coburg, West Canada, became interested in the 1840's in the heating and ventilating of houses and became a recognized authority on the subject. He later applied his idea to railroad cars and developed the Ruttan system of heating and ventilating cars. In the course of his experiments he discovered the importance of moisture in the air and mentioned it in his

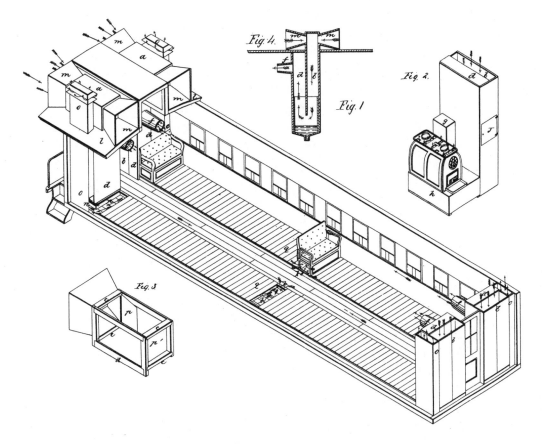

Ruttan system of heating and ventilating cars (patented by Henry Jones Ruttan, January 9, 1866, No. 52009)

patent specifications as one of the " requisites to the effectual ventilation of railroad cars."

In the Ruttan system, the air entered through four " receivers " (m), which were placed in pairs at each end of the roof of the car. From them it was conducted through ducts or " trunks " (b) to shallow water tanks suspended from the floor of the car. In passing over the surface of the water in the tanks, the dust and cinders were removed by the splash, and the clean air then moved upward through ducts (d) to the openings (f) leading into the car. The openings were placed at a height sufficient for the cleaned air to " first visit the faces of the passengers, which is by long odds the most felicitous mode of application." After circulatihg in the car, the air passed into openings (g) under the two center seats and then found its way, in the space between the upper and lower floors, to up drafts in such corner of the car and thence out through cowls (o) in the roof.

In winter the cleaned air from one of the ducts was deflected before it entered the car and was conducted to an air and water chamber (h) under a stove. The stove was provided with tubes in which the air was warmed to the temperature desired. As there was an air duct in each corner of the car, four stoves could be operated if that many were needed.

Ruttan's ventilators were first used in 1856 on the Grand Trunk Railroad of Canada. They were later installed experimentally on a number of railroads in the eastern part of the United States, including the New York Central and the Erie. Ruttan did not patent his idea until January 9, 1866, by which time the railroads had lost interest in such devices and abandoned the use of them.

These primeval air conditioners seem to have been a success from the passengers' point of view, but for some unknown reason they were discarded. Probably the ballasting of the roads reduced the dust to the point where it was no longer a serious problem, or the operation and maintenance of the apparatus were far too costly for the railroads of the time.

After these early experiments, the railroads showed no further interest in air conditioning until 1884, in which year the Baltimore & Ohio fitted a car with a cooling system that consisted of a large icebox built in the front end, in which the entering air was cooled before it passed

Interior of the dining car *Martha Washington*, the first air-conditioned car (by courtesy of the Baltimore & Ohio Railroad)

through ducts to the body of the car. The scheme was not successful, because of the enormous amount of ice required and the poor circulation of the air. In 1906 the idea was revived by the same railroad, and a dining car was equipped with a different type of cooling system using ice. It actually cooled the car, but, as in 1884, the great cost of the ice and the difficulty of keeping the cars supplied made it impracticable.

The next attempt was made in 1925 with a mechanically operated system that did not get past the experimental stage. It was not, in fact, until 1929 that the first really workable method was developed. After testing it in an experimental coach the Baltimore & Ohio equipped the dining car *Martha Washington* with it and operated it successfully. On May 24, 1931, the *Columbian*, consisting of two completely air-conditioned trains, was put on the run between New York and Washington. It was the first complete train in history to be air conditioned.

From the earliest days everyone realized the danger of fire from the

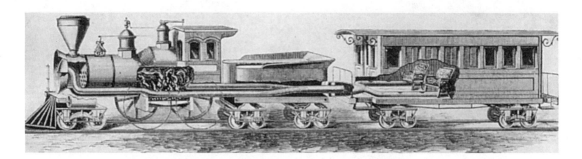

Francis apparatus for heating and ventilating cars
(from the *Scientific American*, October 28, 1868)

stoves in case of an accident, and various attempts were made to heat the cars by other means. Methods were suggested of conveying hot air from the locomotive firebox to the cars, but the difficulty of making a flexible connection in the air duct between the cars and the danger of fire from an overheated duct prevented their use. A method was also devised of circulating hot water through pipes under the car floor, which to a great extent relieved the suffering of the passengers from chilled feet, but it was not until steam from the locomotive's boiler was used that the heating system was perfected. Steam had been considered at an early date, but the danger of scalding the passengers in case of a wreck was as great as the danger of fire from the stoves. This danger was finally overcome by the invention of a valve that reduced the boiler steam to a pressure safe for use in the cars. When, finally, a durable and flexible joint for the steam line between the cars was invented, heating by steam became both safe and feasible. Steam was first used to heat an entire train in the winter of 1887, and soon afterward it came into general use.

~ 6 ~

THE
FIRST
SLEEPING
CARS

The first sleeping cars were simply day coaches from which the seats had been removed and rows of bunks substituted. Some few were later built especially as sleeping cars, but they all followed the day-coach model, and externally there was no difference except, possibly, the words *Sleeping Car* along the side of the car and a coat of extra-bright paint.

The first of these bunk cars was the *Chambersburg*, which was put into service by the Cumberland Valley Railroad in 1836 and used on the night run between Harrisburg and Chambersburg. It was built in Philadelphia, and according to the record that has come down it had a few seats in one end in addition to the berths. After the *Chambersburg* began to run, a number of other railroads put into service sleeping cars that were equipped with bunks, usually built three high along one side of the car with curtains in front. The toilet facilities consisted of a washbasin and a roller towel at one end. At first no bedding other than a hard mattress was furnished; the passengers either supplied their own blankets or, what was more usual, slept in their clothes. At a later date sheets and blankets were supplied. They were stored by day in a

Interior of the first sleeping car, the *Chambersburg* of
1837 (by courtesy of the Pennsylvania Railroad)

box at the end of the car, and at night each passenger took what he
needed and made up his own berth. The bedding was seldom if ever
washed, and the cars were ill kept and dirty. They were only for men
of a tough breed, and women never ventured into them. The usual
charge for a berth was twenty-five cents, and none were reserved.

The berths in the bunk cars were permanent fixtures, and the cars
were in use only at night. But within a few years cars were being built,
or at least equipped, for use as sleeping cars at night and regular passenger service by day. In 1838 the Havre de Grace Railroad (Philadelphia, Wilmington and Baltimore Railroad, now a part of the Pennsylvania) acquired a number of them and, as was the custom in those
days, they were opened to public inspection and the newspapers chroni-
cled the event. The longitudinal seats with which they were furnished
were convertible into two tier berths with a capacity of twenty-four
persons in each car. The cars were put into service on the night of
October 31, 1838, and on the same day the Baltimore *American* carried
a description of their sleeping arrangements:

A press of other engagements having previously prevented our visiting the night cars, just brought from Philadelphia by the Havre de Grace Railroad Company, we availed ourselves yesterday of a little leisure to see and examine them. The arrangement is perfect in its way and will promote the comfort of travelers to a very great degree. During the day the bottoms of the upper tier of berths fold downward so as to form the back of the lower seat and render them as comfortable as can be. Whenever an upper berth is wanted it is only necessary to draw up the back to a horizontal position where it is sustained by an iron catch at each end, take a pillow and blanket from the rack above, made for the purpose, and there is found at once a snug bed. To prevent the possibility of rolling off a strap from the ceiling passes in front of the body of the sleeper and is fastened under the berth. There are, in connection with the above, day cars, for the accommodation of ladies, admirably fitted out. Mr. Imlay deserves infinite credit for his ingenuity and the company are entitled to the thanks of the public for the provision thus made for their comfort.

On November 12 an advertisement appeared in the same paper inviting passengers to take the " night cars which are arranged with berths and other conveniences for the most comfortable night's sleep."

In 1843 the Erie Railroad put into service the Diamond cars, mentioned in a previous chapter. In them the seats were built in pairs facing each other and could be converted into berths by placing a shelf across the space between the two seats. It supported the seat cushions, and the cushions from the backs were placed on the seats (E. H. Mott, *The Story of the Erie* [New York, 1899]). The Diamond cars were more in the nature of reclining-chair cars and were not used for night travel. It was not until the latter 1850's that sleeping cars resembling those of today were invented. Porters were not to be available for some years, and all the inventors of this period stressed the fact that their inventions were so simple in operation that the most inexperienced passenger would have no difficulty changing from seat to berth or back again.

The first of the basic inventions was the car seat and couch invented by Henry B. Myer (sometimes erroneously spelled Meyer) and patented on September 19, 1854. His plan consisted in folding the backs of ordinary car seats to a horizontal position over the arms, without detaching them from the frames, and, when in this position, fastening them so as to form platforms that could be used as berths. The seat cushions were also hinged and could be turned over to cover the space between

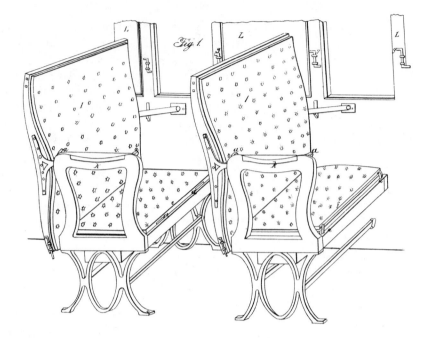

Myer sleeping-car berth (patented by H. B. Myer,
September 19, 1854, No. 11699)

the seats and in this way form lower berths. It was possible by the arrangement to make an unbroken line of berths from end to end of the car. Or, if the passengers preferred, they could "convert their seats into beds capable of accommodating them in a lying position without incommoding the other passengers in the least." Myer preferred ventilation to privacy and did not provide partitions or curtains between or in front of his berths. He later had an interest in the Central Transportation Company, one of the first builders of sleeping cars.

The first convertible car seat of the two-passenger type known to have come into use was the seat and couch invented by Theodore Tuttle Woodruff and patented on December 2, 1856 (Nos. 16159 and 16160). Woodruff designed a car divided into sections, with seats permanently fixed in pairs and facing each other, as in a present-day sleeping car. Two berths, a lower and a middle, were formed by a complicated arrangement from pivoted seat cushions, and a top berth was made up from hinged frames that folded out of the way by day.

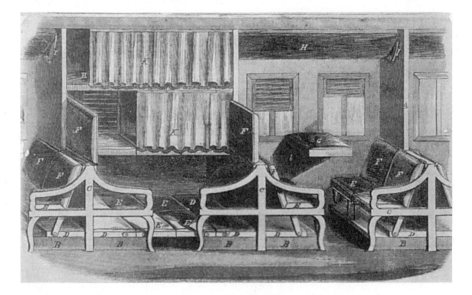

T. T. Woodruff sleeping car (from the *Scientific American, September* 25, 1858)

The lower berth was wide enough for two persons; one person could sleep in the middle berth and one in the top. Curtains were hung at night between and in front of the berths. The Woodruff car was first used on the New York Central in 1858, and by the end of that year it was in service on eight of the western roads. The charge for a berth on the New York Central, and probably on the others, during the next few years was fifty cents.

In 1858 Webster Wagner built his first sleeping cars for the New York Central. There is no record of Wagner having received a patent for a sleeping car, nor, indeed, for any other car, at the time these cars were built, but it is known that his lower berths were formed by simply letting down the backs of the seats to a horizontal position. Two single berths, a middle and a top one, were made from light cane-bottomed frames that were fastened at night to the side of the car and stored under the roof by day. Mattresses and bedding were furnished, and the berths were enclosed by curtains, making what was described at the time as a very comfortable sleeping place.

The longitudinal curtains that were used to partition off the berths provided the passenger with some privacy, but did not protect him from his neighbor. J. B. Creighton undertook to remedy this defect in his patent of September 28, 1858 (No. 21600). " It is necessary," he said in his papers," that there be a partition of some kind to keep the feet of one passenger from protruding into the couch of another, and it is necessary, to effectually prevent this, that the partition should be solid." His invention, in addition to providing solid folding partitions, consisted of a jointed and collapsible frame for suspending two single berths from the roof of the car.

The year 1858 was a fertile one in sleeping-car ideas. Besides Woodruff and Wagner, whose cars came to be widely used, the famous George Mortimer Pullman first appeared as a builder of sleeping cars, and Eli Wheeler received his first patent. In the cars Pullman built for the Chicago & Alton he used some form of the pivoted-back car seat, with upper berths of the platform type. No patent was issued to Pullman or Field at the time, and an exact description of their car seats and berths is lacking, but they were probably an early form of the car seat and berth shown in the Field and Pullman patent of April 5, 1864. This patent was for an improved method of suspending the upper berth from

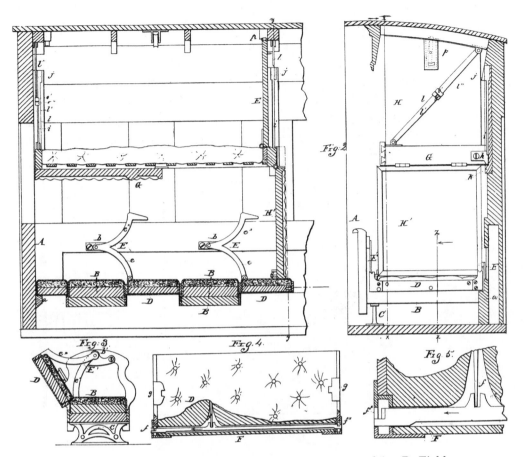

Field and Pullman sleeping car (patented by B. Field and George M. Pullman, April 5, 1864, No. 42182)

the roof of the car and a method of securing the back of the car seat when in its normal position.

The platform or tray type of upper berth, which remained in a horizontal position while being raised or lowered, was a favorite with the inventors of 1858 and thereabouts, and a number were patented within a few years. A few were used in their entirety, but most of them merely furnished certain details for later inventors—for example, the use of counterweights to ease the lowering and raising of the upper berth. A patent for an arrangement of this kind was issued to C. M. Mann on

August 31, 1859 (No. 21352), and counterweights in some form are to be found in many of the designs that followed.

Eli Wheeler's first patent, of August 3, 1858 (No. 21099), contained nothing of particular interest, but his second, of September 20, 1859, was for a sleeping-car seat that had a number of novel features, some of which have survived to this day. The seats were arranged in pairs, as in the Woodruff car, facing each other, but they could not be moved

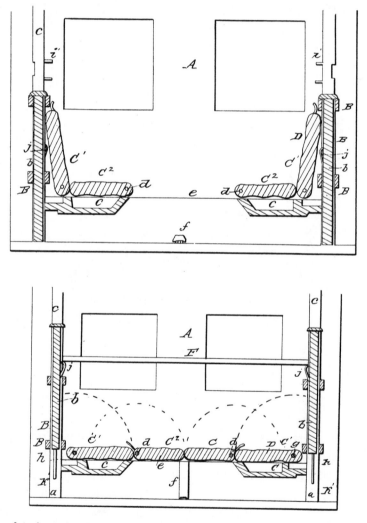

Eli Wheeler sleeping-car berth (patented by Eli Wheeler, September 20, 1859, No. 25499)

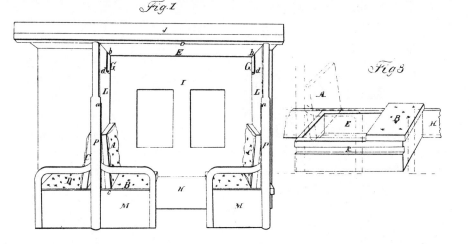

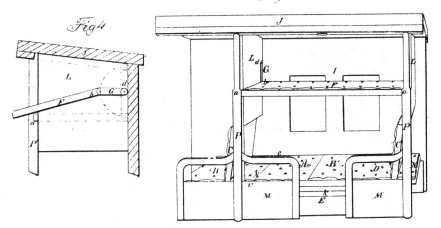

Plymon B. Green sleeping-car berth (patented by
Plymon B. Green, December 21, 1858, No. 22364)

or reversed. The seat cushions were pivoted instead and turned over to
form the lower berth. A space was provided in the back of each seat
into which the sliding partitions could be lowered from between the
berths and stored by day. Wheeler's patent passed through a number
of hands, and somewhere in the course of the various transactions Pullman acquired an interest in it. Its sliding partition later appeared in the
first Pullman car. In 1875 the patent was reissued to Pullman as assignee.

Plymon B. Green, a Chicago photographer, invented a car seat and
couch for which he received a patent on December 21, 1858. At vari-

ous times claims have been put forward that Pullman appropriated Green's invention and used it in his cars, but if there was any appropriating it was actually done by Wheeler. Wheeler, who followed Green, pivoted the back cushion of the seat in forming the lower berth, in the same manner as Green, but there is no similarity in the other features of the two inventions. Green also hinged his upper berth, which may have been the basis of some of the claims, but, except for the use of hinges, the Pullman berth and the Green berth were entirely different.

The upper berth invented by Edward Collins Knight and patented on June 28, 1859, was unique in that its action was automatic. It was suspended from the roof of the car by cords to which counterweights were attached and was balanced so that it would return without assistance to its place under the roof as soon as the passenger relieved it of his weight. In its lowered position it was necessary for the passenger to hold it down by hand or fasten it with a cord. The scheme does not seem to have been a success, and by the following September Knight had changed his ideas and patented an upper berth (No. 25570) that functioned in a directly opposite manner.

This berth was held against the roof of the car by a spring catch which, on being released, allowed the berth to fall until it came to rest on the backs of the seats below, the passenger having to take care to stand from under. Boards that were stored under the seats by day were used at night to span the space between the seats and act as a support for the seat cushions, which were hinged and turned over to form the lower berth. The Baltimore & Ohio entered a contract with Knight in 1862 for the use of his patents, and in 1863 he assigned them to the Central Transportation Company.

In 1861 a car designed by Asa Hapgood was put into service on the Springfield Line between Boston and New York and continued operating until 1868. There is no record of a patent having been issued to Hapgood and little is known about his car except that the seats were convertible into berths and that the cars were divided into sections, six to a side, in each of which there were three berths. The charge for a berth was fifty cents.

The ventilating system in the early sleeping cars consisted of a few stovepipe ventilators in the roof and portholes covered with perforated

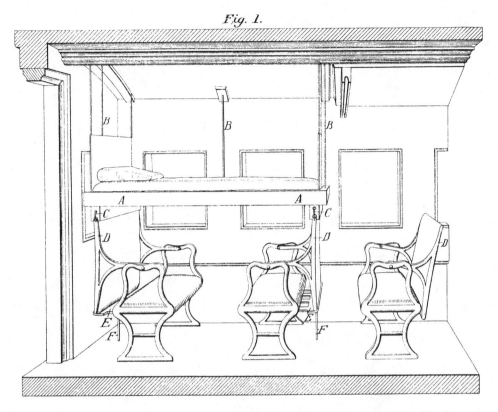

Fig. 1.

E. C. Knight sleeping-car berth (patented by E. C. Knight, June 28, 1859, No. 24563)

zinc shutters in the sides of the car. When the windows were closed, there was little if any circulation of air, and most of the complaints registered by the passengers were about the deadly atmosphere in the cars at night. Webster Wagner no doubt received as many complaints as the other operators of sleeping cars. Having had ample experience with the usual type of ventilators, he devised, in company with Alba Smith, a system, borrowed in part from the inventors of the 1850's, that provided ample openings for the escape of heated air. It changed the appearance of all future passenger cars until the flush roof was revived for use on air-conditioned cars.

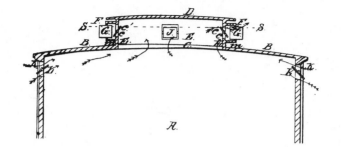

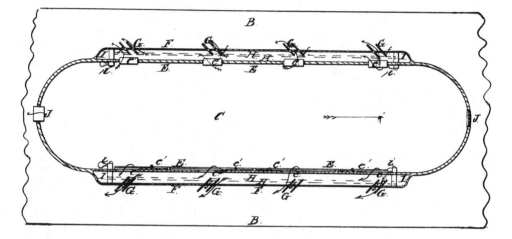

Smith and Wagner car-ventilator (patented by Alba
F. Smith and Webster Wagner, September 23, 1862,
No. 36536)

In the design patented by Wagner and Smith on September 23, 1862,
a section of the car roof was raised above the roof proper, and in the
vertical sides of the raised section a series of openings were formed,
each of which was fitted with a pivoted shutter that could be adjusted to
direct the air currents set up by the motion of the train so as to exhaust
the air from the interior of the car. This was the first appearance of the
raised deck or clerestory car roof, which is still in general use.

On September 19, 1865, Field and Pullman received a patent for a
sleeping car that had some of the features that are still to be found in a

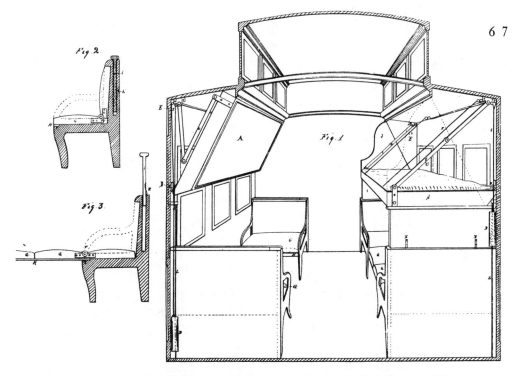

First Pullman sleeping car (patented by George M.
Pullman, September 19, 1865, No. 49992)

standard Pullman sleeper. The seats were in pairs with immovable backs
as in the Wheeler patent, and the Wheeler sliding partition was shown,
although it was not claimed as a part of the invention. The seat cushions
were of the hinged type, but, unlike any previously patented, the back
and the seat cushions were hinged together and moved as a unit when
the seat was made into a berth. The cushions were supported on one
side, when in the berth position, by a device fastened to the side of the
car and on the other by a bar that spanned the space between the seats,
as in the Diamond and Knight cars. The upper berth was hinged to
the side of the car as it is today. Another hinged berth was patented by
Rudolph Dirks in 1859 (No. 24998). It was described by him as "a
peculiar arrangement of hinged boards," but except for the hinges it
had no similarity to the Pullman berth.

The first Pullman car embodying all these new features was put into service on the Chicago & Alton in 1865. In its design Pullman departed from the usual day-coach model and built a car that created a distinct type. The early railroads had borrowed a number of ideas from ships and shipping, and in planning the decorations of his car Pullman did not overlook the public's delight in the elaborate and ornate decorations used at the time in the cabins and saloons of river steamboats. The interior of his first car was finished in black walnut embellished with marquetry, and a number of mirrors were placed in the paneling. The floor was carpeted, and the seats were upholstered in plush.

The body of the car was divided into eight sections, and in addition a washroom and two compartments were built in each end. It cost more than $20,000. Since it was impossible to get all of Pullman's fittings into a car of standard size, the car was built longer, wider, and higher than any standard-gauge car previously constructed. To allow for its increased width, it was necessary for the Chicago & Alton to alter all its platforms and a number of its bridges, and this work was done hastily in the spring of 1865, so that the car could be attached to the Lincoln funeral train at Chicago for the trip to Springfield. It was later used by Grant between Detroit and Galena. As it traveled about the country carrying various notables, the different railroads made the necessary changes to accommodate it. This first car, which was named the *Pioneer*, was followed by others of increasing length and additional comforts. The charge for a berth had risen from the original twenty-five cents to a dollar and a half by the time Pullman entered the field, and he increased it to two dollars.

The Silver Palace cars of the Central Pacific Railroad were owned and operated by the railroad and were in use west of Ogden after the transcontinental railroad was opened. They were painted a bright canary yellow, and the metal fittings of the interior were of white metal to imitate silver, but they were not so elaborately decorated or so luxurious as some of the cars in use on the eastern railroads. The patents under which they were built had been assigned to the Central Pacific Railroad by the Central Transportation Company in 1869 with the understanding that the cars were not to be used east of the Rocky Mountains. The patents included those of T. T. Woodruff, H. B. Myer, E. C. Knight, and Jonah Woodruff.

Interior of a Pullman sleeping car, 1869 (from the *Illustrated London News*, October, 1869)

Jonah Woodruff, a brother of T. T. Woodruff, had been interested in the Woodruff car from its earliest days, and when the Central Transportation Company finally assigned its patents to the Pullman Palace Car Company, he organized the Woodruff Sleeping and Palace Car Company, which was incorporated in May, 1871. He took out four patents between 1867 and 1874, but the principal patents under which his company operated were those issued to Christian E. Lucas in 1875.

In the Lucas car the seats were reversible, with pivoted backs that turned over when they were converted into berths. They were arranged in pairs, with one of them fixed and the other connected to the side of the car by a link which allowed it to be moved far enough to provide space for the mattress. Longitudinal strips of wood or metal were built into the bottom of each mattress to span the space between the seats and to support the weight of the passenger. A Woodruff car is reported by a passenger to have been in service on the Baltimore & Ohio in 1872. It was lighted by candles and had twelve chairs in addition to six sections. The price of a chair was one-half the price of a berth.

Nathan Thompson patented a sleeping car on December 28, 1858 (No. 22462), in which the seats were arranged back to back in two rows down the center of the car, with the passengers seated facing the windows. Similar ideas appeared occasionally among the numerous patents issued at the time, but it was not until after William Flowers had patented his car on September 8, 1874, that a company was organized to build cars of this type. In the Flowers car the seats were in two rows along the center, with an aisle on each side next to the windows. They were built in pairs facing each other, so that the passengers were seated in the usual way. Flowers claimed that his cars were cheaper to build than others, that they were capable of better ventilation, and that they afforded more privacy to the passengers in dressing. In 1881 the Flowers Sleeping Car Company was organized in Bangor, Maine, to build and operate these cars, but it ceased doing business before 1892. The Flowers cars are said to have been in use on some of the New England railroads, but I have been unable to learn where they were operated.

The sleeping cars built for the Hudson River Railroad in 1853 were divided into compartments, and the Pullmans of 1865 had several compartments in addition to the usual berths and seats, so the idea of a

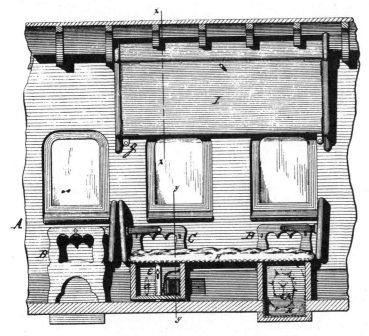

C. E. Lucas sleeping-car berth (patented by C. E. Lucas, February 2, 1875, No. 159428)

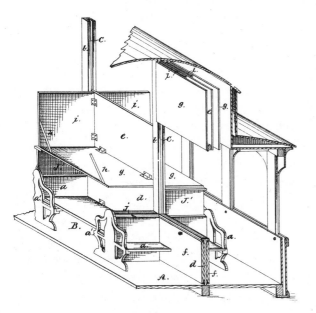

William Flowers sleeping car (patented by William Flowers, September 8, 1874, No. 154790)

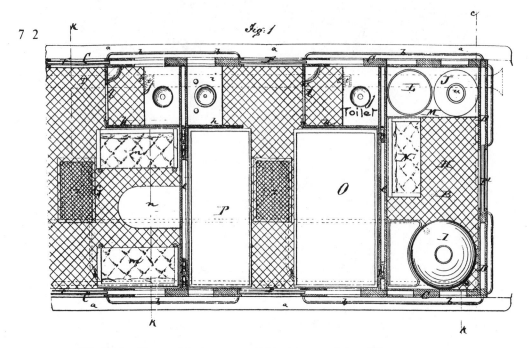

W. D'A. Mann sleeping car, 1872 (patented by W.
D'A. Mann, January 9, 1872, No. 122622)

sleeping or parlor car made up entirely of compartments was not new
when William D'A. Mann received a patent on one on January 9, 1872.
The partitions between the compartments in the Mann car extended
the full width of the car, and the compartments were entered through
doors in the sides, as on the European railroads. There was a small
toilet room in each compartment, and the seats were designed so as to
be convertible into berths that ran at right angles to the direction of
travel.

These cars were first put into service in Europe, as were the cars
Mann patented on January 8, 1878. The latter were also divided into
compartments, but in place of the small toilet rooms there was a corridor reaching from end to end of the car, with a women's dressing
room at one end and one for men at the other. The compartments were
entered from the corridor, and the car from the platforms, which were

enclosed, forming vestibules. The cars were elaborately furnished and decorated and were popular with the traveling public, but because of their limited capacity, a higher rate was charged on them than on ordinary sleeping cars. They were the forerunners of the present-day compartment car and bed car. Mann organized the Mann Boudoir Car Company to build and operate his cars in the United States, and they were put into service on the Springfield Line between New York and Boston in 1883.

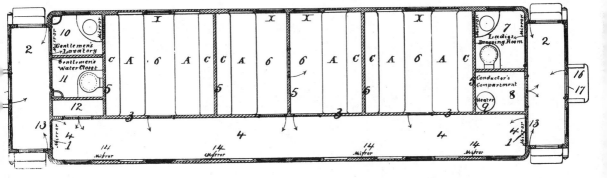

W. D'A. Mann sleeping car, 1878 (patented by W. D'A. Mann, January 8, 1878, No. 198991)

The last sleeping-car company to come into existence, organized to build and operate sleeping cars of a distinct type, was the Monarch Palace Car Company, which was incorporated in 1886 and survived into the 1890's. Its cars are described in its advertisements of 1891 as "embracing the novel design of combining in one car elegant revolving chairs for day use and comfortable springbeds for night use." A sleeping car of this type was patented by J. A. Schmitz on January 3, 1882, and another by R. J. Montgomery on October 4, 1887 (No. 370882).

Combination revolving-chair and sleeping-car berth
(patented by J. A. Schmitz, January 3, 1882, No.
251737)

It has not been possible to identify the patents under which the Monarch Company operated or the railroads on which its cars were used. But the Big Four advertised a combination reclining-chair and sleeping car during the time the Monarch Company was in business. The company also controlled the patents for the Monarch parlor-observation car.

WOODRUFF, WAGNER, PULLMAN, AND MANN

Of the three great builders of sleeping cars who appeared in 1858, Woodruff was the first to get his car into general use, and he was also the first to disappear from the field. His cars were crude, but they were a great advance over the bunk cars they replaced, and by educating the public in the use of the convertible type of car seat, he prepared the way for the luxurious cars that came later.

Theodore Tuttle Woodruff was born in Burrville, New York, on April 8, 1838. At the age of sixteen he was apprenticed to a wagon-builder, and after working at that trade for three years he went into a foundry to learn pattern-making. Later, as a journeyman pattern-maker, he acquired experience in car-building and eventually became master car-builder of the Terre Haute & Alton Railroad at Alton, Illinois. In December, 1856, he received two patents for a convertible car seat, and in 1857 T. W. Wason & Company of Springfield, Massachusetts, built a car for him in which the patented seats were used. This car was first tried on the New York Central in the spring of 1858, and Woodruff traveled with it and personally managed it.

About this time he accidently met Andrew Carnegie on a train and interested him in a model of the car seat that he was carrying with him. Carnegie took him to T. A. Scott, superintendent of the Pennsylvania Railroad, who encouraged him to proceed with his plans of organizing a company to build and operate his cars. When T. T. Woodruff & Company was founded in 1858, Carnegie had a share in it. The Woodruff car was taken off the New York Central when trouble developed between Woodruff and that road, and it was sent to Pittsburgh, where Woodruff was successful in having it adopted by the Pennsylvania for use on the run between Pittsburgh and Philadelphia. It met with considerable success, and by the end of 1858 eight of the western roads had Woodruff cars in service.

In 1862 the Central Transportation Company was incorporated, with Woodruff as the principal stockholder, and in 1863 E. C. Knight and other inventors assigned their patents to the company. Woodruff retained his interest in T. T. Woodruff & Company, which owned or controlled various patents that were used, with restrictions, by the Central Transportation Company, until 1864, in which year he assigned all his interests to O. W. Childs, one of the incorporators of the Central Transportation Company, and retired from the sleeping-car business. The latter company became involved with Pullman in a suit over patent infringements, and in 1870 after costly litigation it assigned its rights in the Knight, Van Houten, and other patents to Pullman's Palace-Car Company. In 1889 the Central Transportation Company combined with the Mann Boudoir-Car Company to form the Union Palace-Car Company, which was absorbed by the Pullman Palace-Car Company in the same year, but some part of it seems to have survived, for the company was not finally dissolved, by court order, until 1899.

After he sold his interest in the sleeping-car business, Woodruff engaged in banking for a number of years and then bought the Morris Iron Company, of Morristown, Pennsylvania. While operating the iron works, he invented a process for making indigo and became interested in a coffee-hulling machine. The latter absorbed his capital, and his business ended in bankruptcy during the depression of 1875. He later invented a steam plow, a surveyor's compass, and a method of propelling ships. He was killed by an express train at Gloucester, New Jersey, on May 2, 1892.

Webster Wagner's success as a builder and operator of sleeping cars was largely due to his association with the Vanderbilts, which assured him from the beginning an exclusive field for his cars on the New York Central and its allied lines. When the opportunity arose, he was able to extend his operations to other roads, but his competitors were barred from his preserves. By license and other means he acquired the privilege of using various improvements in sleeping cars as they developed, and his cars were equipped with the latest gadgets and were as ornately decorated as the taste of the time required. Wagner cars were in regular service at the time the Pullman cars were in their larval state, and the Wagner Palace-Car Company survived until 1899, the year in which Cornelius Vanderbilt died.

Wagner was born at Palatine Bridge, New York, on October 2, 1817. After he had learned the trade of wagon-builder from an older brother, the two of them started a small wagon-manufacturing business, but the venture was not a success, and Wagner withdrew from the business and became station agent at Palatine Bridge. During the time he held this position he devised his sleeping car, and it was with the financial help of Commodore Vanderbilt that he built four cars in 1858. These were put into service on the New York Central, and when they proved successful, Wagner organized the New York Central Sleeping-Car Company, and in 1867 a drawing-room car for day travel was added to the cars it built. In 1869 the Gates Sleeping-Car Company was absorbed. The Gates Company was one of the earliest, if not the earliest, of the sleeping-car companies, and its cars, of the bunk type, were in operation on the Lake Shore Railroad in 1858. Wagner is said to have acquired some valuable patents when he absorbed it, but there is no record of the nature of them.

About 1870 he received permission from Pullman to use Pullman berths in the Wagner cars, with the understanding that he was to confine his operations entirely to the New York Central lines. This arrangement was in effect in 1875, when Pullman's contract with the Michigan Central expired. Wagner, overlooking his obligations, induced the latter railroad to use Wagner cars. Pullman retaliated with an infringement suit for $1,000,000, and the suit went on until testimony was introduced showing a disconcerting similarity between the seats in dispute and those used in the Erie's Diamond cars of 1843. The case was then com-

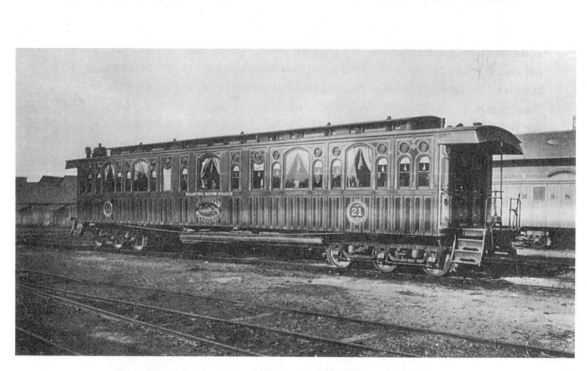

Drawing-room car on the Day Express between Chicago and Cleveland, 1868 (L. S. & M. S. Railway) (by courtesy of the New York Central System)

promised. In 1888 the two companies were in court again in a suit over the Pullman vestibule, which the Wagner Palace-Car Company had appropriated. In this case Pullman was victorious. The battles continued until, at the end of 1899, the year Vanderbilt died, the directors of the Wagner Palace-Car Company voted to discontinue operations, and the company was sold to the Pullman Company.

Wagner was active in New York State politics, and in 1871 he was elected to the state senate. He was killed while riding in one of his own cars in a collision at Sputen Duyvil, New York, on January 13, 1882.

George Mortimer Pullman is popularly credited with the invention of the sleeping car, but, like many other devices that have come into daily use, it really embodies the inventions of a number of men. There is no record of Pullman ever having claimed the honor for himself. He made important mechanical contributions, but the rapid progress of the Pullman car in the public's favor was not due entirely to the design or equipment of the cars. Pullman was pre-eminently an organizer and a natural hotelkeeper, and he applied his talents to the management of his company and the operation of his cars. He was the first to discover that there was a large class of people who were willing to pay a substantial fee for the privilege of traveling in a car that was clean as well as comfortable. From the first, cleanliness was one of the characteristics of the Pullman car.

Pullman was born at Brocton, New York, on March 3, 1831. He attended the local schools until he was fourteen years old, when, his education completed, he started work as a clerk in a small general store in Westfield, New York. After three years there, he joined his brother, who was established in the cabinet-making business in Albion, New York. Here Pullman acquired that knowledge of woodworking in its higher branches that he later used in the design and decoration of his cars. The returns from the cabinet business were not sufficient to support both brothers, and Pullman looked for other employment. At that time the Erie Canal was being widened through Albion, and he entered into contracts to move a number of buildings back from the original edge of the canal to the new one. When this work was finished in 1855, he moved to Chicago, and, profiting by the experience he had gained moving buildings in Albion, he got contracts to raise the level of certain city streets and the adjoining houses and other buildings. In these enterprises he was successful, and besides accumulating a small fortune he attracted attention by his skill and industry.

Like many ingenious mechanics of his time, Pullman conceived an idea for a sleeping car, supposedly while on a rough night journey to Chicago, but unlike the others he had some financial resources and was able to interest the Chicago & Alton in his plans. The railroad supplied as its contribution two day coaches, which Pullman converted into sleeping cars in 1858, and a third, which was converted in 1859. The initial sleeping-car trip was made on the night of September 1, 1859, on the run from Bloomington, Illinois, to Chicago.

The cars met with some success, but were not entirely satisfactory to the railroad, and nothing further was done at the time. In 1859 Pullman went to the mining regions of Colorado, where he ran a general store and during his idle moments worked on his plans for sleeping cars. On his return to Chicago in 1863 he was joined by his friend Ben Field, and together they perfected plans for building the first real Pullman. The car was built on the property of the Chicago & Alton, and the agreement made with the railroad for its use was the beginning of the Pullman system that later covered the entire country.

Pullman's cars made rapid progress in the public's favor, and in 1867 he organized the Pullman Palace-Car Company with its main shops at Palmyra, New York. They were shortly moved to Detroit, and as business expanded, additional shops were established at St. Louis, Wilmington, Delaware, and San Francisco. Finally, the main shops were moved in 1881 to Pullman, Illinois, an entire town that had been built by Pullman on the open prairie outside of Chicago to house his shops and provide model quarters for his workmen. Pullman's company, however, retained complete control of the town, and before long he was painfully surprised to discover that there were some doubts as to his altruism. In 1889, as a protest against the rates charged for gas, water, and house rent, the town voted for annexation to Chicago. Five years later its workmen joined the American Railway Union in large numbers, and in May 1894, a wage dispute with Pullman ended in a strike which incited the destructive railroad strike of that year.

As Pullman extended his business, he came into competition with the small sleeping-car companies that were in operation on different roads, but only a few of them were able to survive for any length of time, once he had perfected his system. The Wagner Palace-Car Company was the last. When it was bought by the Pullman Company in 1899, competition disappeared.

From then until 1944 the business continued without interruption. On May 8 of that year the United States District Court at Philadelphia entered a decree in a government antitrust suit requiring a separation of the sleeping-car business from the other interests of the Pullman group. Pullman Incorporated elected to dispose of the sleeping-car business and made an offer of the sale of it to a group made up of the railroads on whose lines the majority of the sleeping cars were operated. The offer was accepted by the railroad group, and on December 18, 1945, the sale was approved by the court.

Besides his interests in the Pullman Company, Pullman owned the Eagleton Wire Works and was president of the Metropolitan Elevated Railroad of New York City. He died on October 19, 1897.

Interior of a Pullman drawing-room car, 1869 (from the *Illustrated London News*, October, 1869)

William D'Alton Mann, in the course of his long life, engaged in many enterprises, some of which brought him considerable notoriety, but he is probably generally remembered today more as the publisher of *Town Topics* than as an inventor and operator of sleeping cars. By the time he organized his company, Pullman and Wagner were well established, and the tendency in the sleeping-car business was toward a uniform car and service for the entire country, rather than toward innovations in the design of cars.

Mann was born in Sandusky, Ohio, on September 27, 1839. Before he had completed his studies, his career as a civil engineer was cut short by the opening of the Civil War, which he entered in its first year as a captain in the First Michigan Cavalry. In 1862 he organized the Fifth Michigan Cavalry and later the Seventh, and he was in command of the latter regiment at Gettysburg. During the war he invented and patented various improvements to soldiers' equipment and made a fortune from their sale to the federal government.

After the war he settled in Mobile, Alabama, and became a figure in the business life of the city. He acquired and edited the Mobile *Register* and took an active interest in politics. On January 9, 1872, he received a patent for a sleeping car divided by transverse partitions into compartments, and he spent the next ten years in Europe introducing it on the Continent, where it still survives. In 1878 he invented a corridor car and car vestibule, which were used in the same year in a train built in England for service in Russia. On his return to the United States, he organized the Mann Boudoir-Car Company. His cars were put into service on the Springfield Line between Boston and New York in 1883 and became popular with the traveling public, although, because of their limited capacity, a higher rate was charged than on the ordinary sleeping cars. The Mann Boudoir-Car Company became a part of the Union Palace-Car Company in 1889, and was absorbed with it by the Pullman Company. In 1891 Mann purchased *Town Topics* and later founded the *Smart Set*. He died on May 17, 1920.

8

THE
PIONEER
STREAMLINED
TRAIN

The more enlightened railroad-builders realized at an early date that air resistance had some effect on the speed of trains, but at the slow speeds at which all the early railroads operated the effects were not noticeable enough to cause them much concern. Later, as speeds increased, and especially after the railroads were built across the open prairies, with trains exposed to heavy and continuous head and side winds, more attention was given to the subject, and an occasional inventor appeared with a scheme for reducing the air resistance. By the early 1860's air resistance was given in the manuals on railroads as one of the principal obstacles to the operation of trains at high speed.

But such actual experiments as were made pertained more to ships than to trains. What was thus learned was used by S. R. Calthrop in designing the train for which he received a patent on August 8, 1865. Both its ends were pointed, and the whole train, including the locomotive and tender, was covered with a smooth shell with no projections from its sides to interfere with the free flow of air. A false bottom was placed under, and for the full length of, each car to protect the trucks and other projections from the action of the air, and adjoining cars

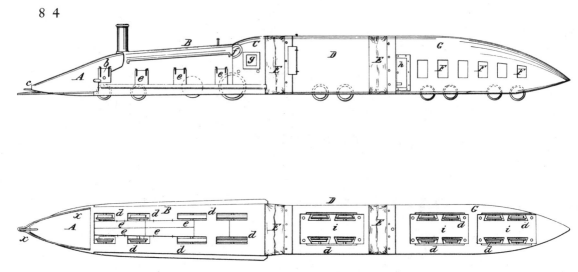

First streamlined train (patented by S. R. Calthrop,
August 8, 1865, No. 49227)

were connected with flexible hoods that enclosed the platforms. The
design as described in the patent had a number of features similar to
those of a modern streamlined train, but as far as is known no actual
train was ever built from it.

During the next twenty years the speed of the best trains did not
average over 30 or 40 miles an hour, and the railroads were not greatly
interested in schemes to increase it. But by the 1890's some of the roads
began to introduce luxury trains running on faster schedules, and a
number of test runs were made in which very high speeds were attained.
In 1893 the Empire State Express of the New York Central covered
a mile at the rate of 112.5 miles an hour, and the next year a train on
the Reading ran 4.8 miles at an average speed of 115.2 miles an hour. In
the next few years long-distance runs were made at high speeds on different roads. At these speeds air resistance became an important factor,
and the inventors of the country tackled the problem again in an effort
to design a train that could defy it.

One of the current inventions materialized into an actual train of six cars. It was the Adams *Windsplitter* designed by Frederick Upham Adams. Sometime in the late 1880's Adams met an inventor who had designed a train for which he claimed a speed of around 950 miles an hour. The train as a whole did not interest Adams, but the retarding effect of the atmosphere aroused his curiosity and started him on an investigation of the subject. After many experiments and long study, he published a book in 1892 (*Atmospheric Resistance in its Relation to the Speed of Trains*; Chicago), which included plans for a streamlined train.

It was built for him at the Mount Clare shops of the Baltimore & Ohio, and on May 8, 1900, it was taken out for a test run on the line between Baltimore and Frederick. (" The Adams *Windsplitter*," by O. Kuhler; *Baltimore & Ohio Magazine*, September, 1936.) The best speed made

Adams *Windsplitter*, 1900 (by courtesy of the Baltimore & Ohio Railroad)

during this trial was 84 miles an hour for 3½ miles. On May 28, with a heavier locomotive, the run from Baltimore to Washington was made in 37½ minutes, which was a record, and during the run several miles were covered at a speed of 87.6 miles an hour. Adams' design for a complete train included a streamlined locomotive, but the importance of this was not realized at the time, and ordinary locomotives were used in the tests. The train did not come up to expectations in either economy of operation or speed, and it was dismantled shortly after the tests.

After the high-speed flurry of the 1890's, the railroads returned to more moderate speeds, and there was little change in the schedules until airplanes became serious competitors for the fast passenger business.

Adams *Windsplitter* on the Thomas Viaduct, Relay, Maryland, 1900 (by courtesy of the Baltimore & Ohio Railroad)

City of Salina, 1934 (by courtesy of the Union Pacific Railroad)

About 1932 the Union Pacific undertook an investigation to determine what steps should be taken to retain its passenger business and bring its equipment into accord with the times. The result was the first modern streamlined train. It was named the *City of Salina*, and was delivered to the railroad on February 12, 1934. After a tour of the country it was put into operation between Kansas City and Salina, Kansas.

In preparing the plans for the *City of Salina*, scientific accuracy in streamlining was assured by a series of tests on wooden scale models in the wind tunnel at the University of Michigan. The train was built by the Pullman Car and Manufacturing Corporation of an aluminum alloy weighing one-third as much as steel of equal strength. It was completely air conditioned, but did not have sleeping accommodations. The 600-horsepower internal-combustion engine was built by the Winton Engine Corporation, and the train carried enough fuel for a run of about 1,200 miles. Before the first train was completed, a larger one was ordered. It became the *City of Portland* and was the first streamliner equipped with sleeping cars. No patents were sought by the Union

Pacific on the new train, and the results of all its experiments were open to any interested railroad.

On April 18, 1934, two months after the *City of Salina* was delivered by her builders, the first Burlington *Zephyr* was christened at Broad Street Station, Philadelphia, and also sent on a tour of the country. This *Zephyr*, like the ones that followed, was built of stainless steel by the Edw. G. Budd Manufacturing Company and was powered by a 660-horsepower Diesel engine. On May 26, 1934, it made a world record by running nonstop from Denver to Chicago, a distance of 1,015 miles, at an average speed of 77.6 miles an hour. On this run it attained a top speed of 112.5 miles an hour. It was put into regular service between Lincoln, Nebraska, and Kansas City on November 2, 1934.

There is hardly a first-class railroad today that does not have some sort of streamlined equipment.

~ 9 ~

A NOTE
ON
STANDARD
TIME

Before the days of the railroads the country was made up of communities that were more or less isolated from one another. Travel between them was slow and uncertain, and there was no business carried on in which the smaller divisions of time were important factors. Each community fixed its local time according to custom, usually by the sun, and no one was affected or even knew if the clocks in the neighboring towns were either ahead or behind his own.

With the coming of the railroads, and later the telegraph, time became of more importance in daily life, but it was not until the railroads were running on regular schedules that the confusion arising from the diverse systems of time became a matter of concern to anyone. It was then largely a railroad problem, and in an effort to solve it the roads devised systems of their own, but as each road adopted a different system, and the long ones several, their attempts at a solution only added to the confusion. In each city there were at least two systems of time in use, the local and the railroad, and if a number of railroads entered the city, there was an additional system for each road.

At Buffalo the New York Central time was twenty minutes ahead of Buffalo local time, and the Lake Shore time was fifteen minutes behind. Baltimore was three minutes ahead of Washington. Batteries of clocks erected in the principal railroad stations were set to show the local time, the railroad time, and the time in the largest cities along the line. Gadgets were sold on which the various times could be quickly calculated. Everyone recognized the need for a uniform system for the entire country, and different schemes were proposed, but little was done until after the first railroad to the Pacific was in operation and the problem became acute.

Among the schemes proposed was one by Charles Ferdinand Dowd, A. M., Ph. D., in a pamphlet he published in 1870 entitled, "A System of National Time for the Railroads." That system with some modifications, is the one now in use. Dowd was born in Madison, Connecticut, in 1825. He graduated from Yale in 1853 and shortly afterwards embarked on his career as an educator. In 1868 he was appointed principal of the Temple Grove Ladies Seminary at Saratoga Springs, New York, and he remained in that position for thirty-five years. He was a methodical person, and the confusing time standards then in use were to him entirely without reason. As a diversion he made a study of the subject and finally developed the system proposed in his pamphlet.

His original idea was to divide the country into four sections on meridian lines, each section to cover fifteen degrees of longitude or one hour in time, with the meridian of Washington as the primary meridian. It was later found desirable to make certain modifications in the boundary lines, so as to avoid having them pass through cities, and to change the primary meridian from Washington to seventy-five degrees west of Greenwich. The value of his plan was immediately recognized by the railroads, but at the time they were engaged in wars over rates and other matters and were not in a mood for co-operation. The country as a whole was apathetic. Each community took a certain pride in its local time and resisted all efforts to make even minor adjustments.

But Dowd was not to be discouraged, and for twelve years after 1870 he traveled around the country attending railroad conventions and promoting his plan wherever he could find an audience. The press was generally in favor of Dowd's idea and carried on a campaign explaining the advantages of a national system. Gradually opposition lessened.

The American Association for the Advancement of Science, the American Metrological Society, and the American Society of Civil Engineers urged the adoption of Dowd's plan. In 1879 Sir Sanford Fleming, chief engineer of the Canadian Pacific, proposed a similar system for the entire world. Finally, in 1883, the American Railway Association, representing the management of 78,000 miles of railroad, adopted the Dowd plan, and it was put into effect by the railroads on November 18, 1883, with little inconvenience to anyone.

In recognition of his services, Dowd received annual passes on all the railroads of the country. He was killed by a train on a crossing at Saratoga, New York, November 12, 1904.

~ PART II ~

ACCOUNTS BY CONTEMPORARY PASSENGERS

Imlay type of car, 1832 (by courtesy of the Columbia University Libraries)

IN THE DAYS BEFORE THE LOCOMOTIVE

[From the New York *Gazette*, May, 1830]

The railroad, which already passes several miles beyond Ellicotts' Mills [fifteen miles from Baltimore], is a most delightful and useful mode of conveyance. The scenery is of the most picturesque character and when, in June, the locomotives are in operation it must attract the attention of all travelers. The car in which I took my passage to Ellicotts' Mills in May contained twenty-two passengers, drawn by one horse, and the time in going the thirteen miles was one hour and a quarter. By the first of July the locomotives will be in operation, when the same distance will be traveled in thirty minutes.

THE EARLY REFRESHMENT ROOMS

[From *A Diary in America*, Captain Frederick Marryat (Philadelphia, 1840), pp. 9-10]

Of all traveling, I think that by railroad the most fatiguing. After a certain time the constant coughing of the locomotive, the dazzling of the vision from the rapidity with which objects are passed, the sparks and ashes which fly in your face and on your clothes become very annoying; your only consolation is the speed with which you are passing over the ground. The railroads are not fenced on the sides so as to keep the cattle off them and it appears as if the cattle who range the woods are very partial to take their naps on the roads, probably from their being drier than the other portions of the soil. It is impossible to say how many cows have been cut into atoms by the trains.

At every fifteen miles of the railroads there are refreshment-rooms. The cars stop, all the doors are thrown open, and out rush all, the passengers like boys out of school, and crowd round the tables to solace themselves with pies, patties, cakes, hard-boiled eggs, hams, custards and a variety of railroad luxuries too numerous to mention. The bell rings for departure, in they all hurry with their hands and mouths full, and off they go again until the next stopping-place induces them to relieve the monotony of the journey by masticating without being hungry.

The Utica Railroad is the best in the United States. The general average of speed on the other roads is from fourteen to sixteen miles an hour, but on the Utica they go much faster.

A TOUR OF THE EASTERN STATES

[From *Notes on the United States of North America during a Phrenological Visit in 1838-39-40*, George Combe (Philadelphia, 1841), I, 263, 281; II, 71, 88, 167, 299]

This morning, February 16, 1839, at eight o'clock we left Philadelphia and traveled in large and comfortable cars warmed by stoves to Baltimore. The railroad consists of a single track; the distance is ninety-four miles and although we suffered considerable detention by the bridge over the Schuylkill having been lately carried away by a flood and not yet restored, we arrived at 3 P.M. There is a ladies' car in each train, appropriated for ladies and the gentlemen who are traveling with them. It is divided into two apartments and a place of retirement is added. This is a great accommodation, particularly when children are in the party.

On February 18 we left Baltimore at nine o'clock in the morning and traveled to Washington by railroad. We left Washington on February 23 at six in the morning by the railroad, arrived at Baltimore at half past eight, breakfasted, and started at nine by the railroad for Philadelphia. The axle of the baggage-car broke and we were detained for two hours. Nothing could exceed the good humor with which the passengers submitted to the loss of time while the luggage was transferred into the passengers' cars. The trunks and packages were thrown about and dashed against each other on the ground most recklessly, yet this is one of the best managed railroads in the Union. Mr. Newkirk, the president of the company, told me that in engaging all the men employed by the railroad company it is stipulated that they shall practice habitual temperance and that by rigidly acting on these stipulations no serious accident has occurred since the railway was opened in 1838. We arrived at Philadelphia at 6 P.M.

The running of the railroad cars on Sunday from Philadelphia to Columbia is announced and apologized for as indispensable to overtaking the greatly extended Spring trade of this season and a promise is given that the arrangement is only temporary, with a view of forwarding an accumulating mass of goods. In the Eastern States the steamboats and stages, except the mails, do not run on Sundays, but there are morning and evening trains on the railroads for passengers.

My phrenological labors being terminated for the season, we resolved to visit Lake George, Niagara and Canada, and this morning, March 24, at seven o'clock, embarked on board the *Avon* for West Point. . . . After leaving Ballston Spa by the railroad the locomotive engine became unserviceable and the train quietly stood still. Every car poured forth its company in alarm, like bees issuing from their hives on a serious assault. The passengers pushed the whole train backwards about a third of a mile to a passing point, when the engine was run off the track and a messenger was dispatched to Ballston, three miles distant, for aid. After waiting an hour one horse appeared and we proceeded forward at a snail's pace. . . . The Americans are certainly remarkable for good temper, for although there was ground for provocation in the slender supply of horse power, the numerous company displayed the most exemplary patience and good humor. After advancing four miles with one single horse we obtained three and at last after dark arrived at Schenectady.

The railroad from Syracuse to Auburn was opened on June 5 and we traveled on it the third morning of its operation. It was not enclosed and the domestic animals along the line had not yet become accustomed to the appearance of the locomotive engines and trains. It was a curious study to mark the effects of our train upon them as it rushed past. The horses in the fields generally ran away, the sheep and lambs fled in terrible agitation, and the swine early took alarm and tried to run before us. Fortunately, none of these animals ventured on the railroad and we arrived at Auburn, distance 26 miles, in one hour and ten minutes without accident or detention. In a separate car were two stout rascally-looking convicts chained together, going to Auburn State Prison. They were merry and reckless and came out at the half-way station to have their last supply of tobacco and whisky before entering on the life of temperance that awaited them in jail.

At Auburn we met a family from Boston traveling westward and along with them hired an exclusive extra or stage coach seated for nine persons and drawn by four horses. We started at half past nine in the morning and arrived at Canadaigua at 8 P.M.

We proceeded westward to Batavia and Lockport. There we found a railroad which carried us to the Falls of Niagara, where we arrived on June 21. On June 25 we left Niagara Falls at half past two P.M. in a railroad car and arrived at Buffalo at 4 P.M. This railroad runs nearly along the right bank of the Niagara river the whole way to Buffalo, and affords admirable views of the scenery. We left Buffalo on June 27 at 9 A.M. in a railroad car on our return to Niagara Falls. It thundered and rained plentifully and the locomotive engine could not drag us forward. Its wheels continued revolving but slipt on the wet rails and we stood motionless. This railroad is twenty-three miles in length and has ascents in some places exceeding seventy feet in the mile (1.32%). After many stops, we obtained horses and at half past two o'clock reached Niagara Falls. We did not remain in the village but entered a railroad train for Lewistown, where we arrived at a quarter past four P.M.

.   .   .   .   .   .

On October 29 we left Springfield and started for Worcester by the railroad, which has been opened since we traveled to Springfield a month ago. Yesterday a stray horse had its legs and head cut off on this railroad by the engine and the night before a carter had left a cart with stones standing on the track against which a train loaded with merchandise had run in the dark and been smashed to pieces. We hoped to be more fortunate and were so; but, although we encountered no danger, our patience was sufficiently tried. About ten miles from Springfield we came to a dead stop and the whole train stood motionless for three hours, enlivened only by occasional walks in the sunshine and visits to a cakestore, the whole stock of eatables in which was in time consumed, the price of them having risen from hour to hour in proportion to the demand.

The cause of our detention was the non-arrival of the train from Worcester, which, from there being only a single track of rails, could pass our train here and nowhere else. We heard nothing of its fate and expected it to arrive every minute till four o'clock, when at last an express on horseback came up and announced that it had broken down but that it was now cleared off the rails and that we might advance. Again I admire the patience and good humor of the American passengers which never forsook them in all this tedious detention.

At 6 P.M. we arrived at Worcester but here found ourselves in another fix. The afternoon train from Boston does not arrive until 7 P.M. and we could not proceed to the city until it appeared. It was now dark and for another hour and a half the passengers sat with exemplary patience in the cars. At half past seven we started again and arrived in Boston about ten o'clock, with pretty good appetites, as we had breakfasted at half past seven in the morning and been allowed no meal since that hour. The car was seated for fifty-six passengers and contained at least thirty. There was no aperture for ventilation and when night came on the company insisted on shutting every window to keep out the cold. A few who, like us, preferred cool air to suffocation congregated at one end where we opened two windows for our relief.

·   ·   ·   ·   ·   ·

On May 1 we left Harrisburg at seven o'clock in the morning by a railroad for Philadelphia. The country through which it passed is all cleared, highly fertile, well cultivated and possesses much natural beauty. At 1 P.M. the engine was allowed to run off the track and we lost two hours before it could be restored to its place by means of tackle and a multitude of men. No injury was done to it or any of the passengers but we had not proceeded far when the engine stood still. All the coals had been consumed and the engineer had supplied their place with green oak which would not burn. At last a baggage-train came up and pushed our train before it to the next station, where we got a supply of combustible fuel. The engine then performed its duty well and at 7 P.M. we arrived at Philadelphia three hours behind the usual time.

During all these delays, the result of sheer carelessness, not an angry or discontented word was heard from the passengers, who were numerous. The railway train from Philadelphia to New York started at 5 P.M. and we should have arrived an hour before that time instead of two hours after it. Many individuals who had urgent business and appointments in New York found their plans deranged, yet they bore the disappointment with good humor.

✑ 1 8 3 9 ✑

FROM BOSTON TO HARRISBURG

[From *The Eastern and Western States of America*, J. S. Buckingham (London, n. d.), I, 327, 332, 333, 346, 347, 470, 537]

We left Providence for New Haven, Connecticut, on December 19, 1839, going first to Boston and then by the railroad cars to Worcester. The snow lay in many places from two to three feet deep on the ground, but as the road had been cleared since its fall by snow ploughs and extra engines, employed for that purpose, our progress was scarcely at all impeded. The weather was extremely cold but the cars were fitted up with so much comfort, having a stove in the center of each with a large fire, carpets and rugs for the feet and cushions for the seats, that we felt no inconvenience from the air. Our journey from Boston to Worcester was 44 miles, the fare two dollars and the time occupied was about three hours. We stopped at ten different stations to put down and take up passengers and at each of these were comfortable and well furnished waiting-rooms for ladies and gentlemen separately, with ample refreshments for those who needed them. All the appointments of the railroad appeared to be excellent.

We left Worcester on the morning of December 20 at 10 o'clock by the railroad train for Springfield and the delightfully commodious and well warmed cars and the neatly arranged station houses at which we stopped made our journey even more agreeable today than yesterday. The distance is about fifty miles, the fare two and a quarter dollars and the time taken about three hours. We left Springfield at two o'clock in the afternoon in a wretched vehicle called the Hartford stage. We were five hours in going a distance of 27 miles and after the luxurious traveling in the swift and well warmed railroad cars it was the more disagreeable by contrast.

A railroad having been opened only a week ago from Hartford to New Haven, we left Hartford at two in the afternoon of December 21 for that place. If we had not been informed that the train had been running a week between these two cities we should have thought it was the first day of its being opened from the large crowds of people assembled to see it set out. The greatest number of these were from the country, though some were from the town, and they formed a continuous line standing on the edge of the overhanging embankments on each side of the road and then in separate groups, the whole extending for a mile at least from the starting point. The cars were neither so elegant nor so commodious as those on the Massachusetts line from Boston to Springfield, nor had they the comfort of fires in stoves. Their speed was not so great, as we were nearly three hours in going 38 miles, the fare being two dollars.

.   .   .   .   .   .

On Tuesday, February 4, 1840, we left Philadelphia for Harrisburg. We left at seven in the morning by the railroad cars, and, crossing the Schuylkill river by the bridge, were drawn up the inclined plane over which the railroad ascends by a stationary-engine, but not at a very rapid rate. The cars were dirty and incommodious, so that our journey did not afford us much pleasure. After passing several stations and villages we reached Lancaster at two P.M., the distance being 70 miles, the time occupied 7 hours and the fare two dollars and a half each. The railroad from Philadelphia to Lancaster is a work of the State, is well executed and deemed perfectly safe.

From Lancaster to Harrisburg it is the property of a private company and has been so badly constructed that accidents are continually happening on it by the cars getting off the track, by upsetting and by other modes by which passengers are often injured and sometimes killed. The class of persons journeying on this road were inferior in appearance and manners to any we had before met in similar conveyances. The men especially were dirty, vulgar, clamorous and even rude to a degree that we had not before witnessed in our journey. We reached Harrisburg about six o'clock, having been four hours coming a distance of less than forty miles, and the fare was two dollars.

From Harrisburg we returned to Lancaster and passed a week there very agreeably. We left Lancaster on our return to Philadelphia on February 19, 1840. The frosts having broken up and all the heavy snow on the ground melted, the road was in the most miry condition possible and in some places the rails were nearly covered with mud. So much extra caution was necessary in this state of things that we could not proceed at a greater rate than about eight miles an hour and even then we were thrown off the track several times and on each occasion getting the engine and cars on again was a work of considerable delay and difficulty. Added to this the interruptions were perpetual from our overtaking on the same line of rails freight-trains going slower than we were and for which it was necessary to retard our speed until we came to a turn-out. It was quite dark when he reached Philadelphia and we thought it the most disagreeable journey by railroad we had ever performed, though we were told that we ought to congratulate ourselves on not having been upset when thrown off the track or detained for eight or ten hours before we could get in again, which had been the case of the cars on the two preceding trains, in one of which several passengers were wounded in an upset and in the other they were detained all night upon the road and arrived only at sunrise on the following morning.

∽ 1 8 4 0 ∾

AN INHUMAN CONDUCTOR

[From *Civilized America*, Thomas Colley Grattan (London, 1859), pp. 161, 162]

March, 1840. On quitting the steamboat at Newcastle we took the railroad for twenty-two miles to Frenchtown which thus connects the Delaware and Chesapeake Bays. We had made about two-thirds of our journey when at one of the road crossings a violent jolt accompanied by a loud crash made all the passengers start and considerably alarmed some of them. The continued rapidity of our movement, however, satisfied all that no accident had occurred to the cars, and in a quarter of an hour the train stopped close to the water side at Frenchtown. As we stepped out I went up to the conductor and engineer, who stood together on the platform of the locomotive, and inquired the cause of the sudden shock we had experienced.

"Well, it was in going over a chaise and horse," replied one of them cooly.

"There was no one in the chaise?" asked I, anxiously.

"Oh, yes, there were two ladies."

"Were they thrown out?"

"I guess they were and pretty well smashed up, too."

"Good God! and why didn't you stop the train? Can't you send back to know what state they're in?"

"Well, mister, I recon' they're in the State of Delaware; but you'd better jump into the steamer there or you are like to lose your passage."

With these words the conductor turned to some other inquirer.

Many of the passengers agreed with us that it was inhuman of the conductor not to have stopped the train and look after the injured persons. Others remarked that it wouldn't have done any good and that the train was obliged to be on time or have delayed the steamer for ten minutes or more. This was unanswerable; the subject dropped. But a few days afterward I saw in a Baltimore paper a paragraph stating that one of the ladies had been killed, the other badly wounded, the horse smashed and the chaise broken to pieces. The miracle was that the train was not shaken off the track.

৩৩ 1 8 4 6 ৩৩

SNOWBOUND

[From *The Western World; or, Travels in the United States in 1846-47*, Alex. Mackay (London, 1850), pp. 30, 36, 148, 151, 163, 164]

In addition to the round-about journey by sea, the city of New York is approached from Boston by three different routes, each of which is a combination of railway and steamboat traveling. The Long Island Railway being blocked by snow, I selected the route by Norwich in preference to that by Stonington, the former curtailing the sea voyage by thirty miles, a serious consideration, as the navigation of the Sound was then rather perilous owing to the masses of ice with which it was obstructed.

As there was then only one train a day for the West and as for the first forty miles two railways were blended into one, the bustle and confusion which occurred at the station before starting was perfectly indescribable. Everybody was getting to the wrong car and everybody's luggage into the wrong van. At length, after a hubbub which would have been more amusing had it been less intense, the long heavy train started at four P.M. for Worcester.

The carriage in which I found myself seated consisted of one great compartment constructed to accommodate sixty people. It was like a small church on wheels. At either end was a door leading to a railed platform in the open air, and from door to door stretched a narrow aisle on either side of which was a row of seats, wanting only bookboards to make them look exactly like pews, each being capable of seating two reasonably sized persons. The car was so lofty that the tallest man present could promenade up and down the aisle with his hat on.

In Winter two or three seats are removed from one side to make way for a small stove and as I was rather late in taking my place the only vacant seat I could find was one adjoining this portable fireplace. My immediate companion was a gentlemanly looking man under forty and directly opposite him sat a lady of about two hundred and fifty pounds weight, whose traveling stock consisted of a carpet bag almost as plump as herself, which, as she was bringing herself to a comfortable bearing, she consigned to the safekeeping of the gentleman who sat beside me. He could not put it on the floor which was moist with expectoration nor could he put it on the stove which was already getting red hot, so he had no alternative but to carry it the whole night upon his knee, as the ladies are used to such attentions in America.

Finding the heat of the stove uncomfortable, I repaired to one of the platforms attached to the car, where I enjoyed myself in the open air, smoking a cigar and observing the country through which we passed. I had not been long engaged in such reflections when from the next car emerged the conductor, who is in America a peripatetic functionary.

Interior of a Baltimore & Ohio car, 1861 (from the
Illustrated London News, April 6, 1861)

Having received my ticket, he was about to enter the car I had just
quitted when he stopped short and, having permitted his quid to change
sides in his mouth, he observed that it was "tarnation cold" and
inquired if I preferred standing where I was to being seated inside.
"It's a poor choice between being frozen and being roasted," I observed.
He looked at me again and then intimated that he was merely acting
as a friend in telling me I would be safer inside.

"Is there any danger?" I inquired.

"We do sometimes run off the rail, that's all," said he without the
slightest emotion and then passed into the car. I preferred a slow broil
by the stove to being crushed to death and repaired to my place and
submitted to it until the train reached Worcester.

For some minutes after we arrived it appeared to me as if Bedlam had been let loose upon the station, or dépôt, as it is universally called in America. To give a true picture of the confusion—the rushing to and fro—and the noise with which all this was accompanied is impossible. Some pounced upon the refreshment-room as if they fancied it the up-train and in danger of an immediate start; others flew about frantically giving orders which there was no one to obey; while by far the greater number were assuring themselves of the safety of their baggage. This was very necessary inasmuch as the line here branched off into two; the one proceeding to Albany and the other to Norwich en route to New York.

It is by no means an uncommon thing for a passenger to find that his baggage has from this point taken an independent course for itself. This sometimes arises from the baggage being put into the wrong car and at others from the cars themselves being put on the wrong line. Sometimes the separations are most heart-rending, husbands and wives, parents and children being sent off in different directions. This was the case with a lady in the carriage immediately behind that in which I sat. She had been torn from both her husband and her handbox and consoled herself by abusing the conductor, until at last he was goaded into telling her that she had no business to get into the wrong train; from which he derived but little satisfaction as she insisted the whole way that it was the train that was going wrong.

Detached from the Albany train, we were soon on our way to Norwich, led thither by an asthmatic locomotive which went wheezing and puffing along at the rate of twelve miles an hour over the slippery rails. Although nearly sixty people were packed closely together the utmost silence pervaded the car. One by one the company dropped into temporary forgetfulness and before we had been an hour from Worcester two-thirds of them were asleep. A solitary lamp burned at one end of the car and its sickly light fell upon the faces of the sleepers. A company of sleepers is a powerful opiate, nor was I long in feeling its influence, which, aided by the hot stifling air within the car, soon numbered me among them.

I awoke in an agony of perspiration and found the stove, which was within three feet of me, red-hot. I could stand these species of torture no longer and, determined to run all risks, immediately sought refuge in the fresh air. The train whisked over the face of the country like a huge rocket, the wood fire of the engine throwing up a shower of sparks which spread into a broad golden wake behind us. On the platform of the adjoining car I found a fellow traveler who like myself had sought refuge from the heat.

We suddenly came to a halt under a sort of shed which I was informed was the Norwich station. We were still eight miles from Alleyn's Point, where we were to take the steamer, and were soon informed by the conductor that we must stop at Norwich until news of her arrival should reach us. As we might be detained till morning we all scrambled to the nearest hotels.

．　　　．　　　．　　　．　　　．　　　．

My destination on leaving New York was Philadelphia. We were conveyed across the Hudson to Jersey City, on arriving at which the passengers jumped in crowds upon the floating ship, where we landed and fled. I followed the breathless and panting crowd into a large unfinished building which I found to be the railroad station. Once within the station, the hurry-scurry if possible increased; men jostling each other and rushing in at every available aperture into the cars like so many maniacs. On venturing inside one of the cars I discovered the cause of the tumult. It appears that in Winter there is a choice of seats, the preferable ones being such as are not too near or too far from the stove and the race was for these seats.

On the previous night there had been a severe storm accompanied by a heavy fall of snow. As the line was buried in the snow three powerful locomotives were attached to the train. The first of these was preceded by an enormous snow plough, an indispensable feature in the Winter appanages of an American railroad. We started at a slow and cautious pace and for the first few miles encountered no difficulty, the snow having lain lightly as it fell. We soon quickened our pace therefore when the sturdy plough did its work nobly.

Between Newark and New Brunswick nothing particularly occurred with the exception that the difficulties which the snow interposed to our progress increased as we proceeded. It no longer lay softly on the ground but was drifted across the line. Through some of these drifts we made our way with difficulty, at one plunge, the whole train sustaining a shock in the operation like that given to a ship struck by a heavy sea. Others were more formidable, bringing us to a sudden stop in our career when the train would back and rush at them again until by successive efforts the obstacle was overcome. When more than usual force was required, in tender mercy to the passengers who were sometimes thrown all in a heap by these operations into the forepart of their cars, the train would be detached and the locomotives set at it themselves.

It was exciting and amusing enough so long as it occasioned us no serious detention, but just as we were approaching New Brunswick station we ran into a tremendous drift with such force as to baffle all our efforts to get out of it. We anxiously watched the progress of every effort made for our relief until the chilling intelligence was conveyed to us that the fires had all been extinguished in the locomotives and that the water had become frozen in the boilers. There was nothing left for us but to seek the station the best way we could, which we did by making a detour of the drift and wading sometimes up to the middle in snow. On gaining it, we found a large comfortless room leaving but little to choose between it and the cars which we had left.

Seeing how the case was, I made my way to the nearest hotel but the beds had all been pre-engaged so back again I scrambled in the dark through the snow to the station, where I found many loading themselves with billets of wood, others provided with kettles full of hot water and others with bottles of spirits with glasses and sugar. I inquired of a fellow passenger where the orgy was to take place and he informed me that they had just made up their minds to make a comfortable night of it in the beleaguered cars. We were soon once more seated in our respective cars with brisk fires in their stoves and a constant intercourse was kept up between us and the barroom at the station.

We were not wanting in comfort. I slept fitfully during the night as did most of my fellow sufferers. When morning broke we emerged with difficulty from our prison and again sought the hotel, where we breakfasted and remained until nearly evening. In the meantime every appliance was brought to clear the line but it was seven o'clock before we finally quitted New Brunswick. In three hours more we were on the left bank of the Delaware and crossed by ferry to Philadelphia.

For two miles out of Philadelphia on the way to Baltimore you are drawn at an exciting trot by a number of horses. Emerging from a small, cramped station in Market street you proceed along a number of streets, the cars being so constructed as to enable them without diminishing speed to be whipped round the street corners with perfect safety. You have to cross the Schuylkill by a long covered bridge before you succeed in your search for a locomotive.

This civic proscription of railway engines may appear very unreasonable but it is a necessary piece of municipal policy in America, where every town ranks among its more prominent qualities a very high degree of inflammability. The locomotives burn nothing but wood and they are constantly attended by a formidable train of sparks and sometimes amuse themselves on the way by setting fire to a barn, a hayrick and the like, and when they have nothing else to do burning down a fence. Such customs would soon make Philadelphia too hot for them, and therefore their exclusion.

A journey by railway south of Philadelphia and indeed south of the Hudson has many things about it that are disagreeable to the stranger. It is then that he is brought into close contact with tobacco-chewing. Both in New England and in New York tobacco-chewing is a habit by far too prevalent, but this plague in American life only begins to show itself in its detestable universality after he has crossed the Hudson on his way South. A New York railway-car is a clean affair as compared to one on the line between Philadelphia and Baltimore, or more particularly between the latter and the termination of railway traveling in North Carolina. It frequently happens that the seats, the sides of the car, the window hangings, where there are any, and sometimes the windows themselves are stained with the pestiferous decoction.

It had never been my lot to encounter such a hubbub as saluted us on entering the station in Baltimore. There was not a hotel in town that was not represented by one or two Negroes who did the touting for it, each having the name of his boniface displayed on a band around his hat.

I left Baltimore by the late night train for Washington. For two-thirds of the way we went on smoothly enough, but when within ten miles of Washington a violent jerk to the whole train appraised us that we had run against something, not however, sufficiently formidable to bring us to a sudden halt or to dislodge us from the line. The engineer gradually slackened speed and on stopping the train we discovered that we had run against a cow which had been lying on the line.

"I can stand a hog but them cows are the devil to pay," said the stoker as he proceeded with the help of some others to drag the carcass off the engine and deposit it by the side of the line.

It was two in the morning when we reached Washington. A more miserable station than we were ushered into can scarcely be conceived.

꙳⊙ 1 8 4 9 ⊙꙳

COWS ON THE WEST CHESTER LINE

[From *Two Years on the Farm of Uncle Sam*, Charles Casey (London, 1852), pp. 215, 216]

The railroads give a subject for wonder; in many of the cities the tracks are laid right along the streets and the cars come into the heart of the city and there is seldom an accident. In passing through villages the line is usually through the center of the principal street and in the country the crossing roads have no protecting gates and watchmen. There is simply a large board put up on two posts on which is written Look Out For the Locomotive, or Look Out For the Cars When the Bell Rings. In some instances the trains are detached from the engine and each car drawn in by horses, as in New York, but in other instances the engine brings the cars into the city. Cattle repeatedly get on the track and are sometimes run over.

On the West Chester line I remember once on looking ahead seeing three cows on the track about 100 yards off. The driver sprung the whistle and immediately they commenced running straight on the line. Two were young and plunged sideways off and escaped, but the other we gained on fast, never slacking speed. Another moment, and crunch, jolt, crunch and the poor creature lay a bruised and bleeding mass. I appealed to the conductor but he only observed that people should keep their cattle off the track.

There seems to be an intuitive fraternity between most of the animals and the engine. You will see teams of young horses drawn up close to the train looking as familiar as if it was an old stable mate and its gruff voice does not excite them in the least. While the train stands, dogs run among the wheels and I have seen pigs come and luxuriate on the tar and grease that oozed from the wheel-boxes and yet they seldom or never receive an injury.

∽ 1 8 5 0 ﬞ

TRICKED AT NIAGARA

[From *A Glimpse at the Great Western Republic*, Lieut. Col. Arthur Cunynghame (London, 1851), pp. 19, 20, 30, 44]

The railroad cars throughout the United States, with the exception of what we should call a sort of luggage-van for immigrants, seldom or ever have more than one class. They are built somewhat after the fashion of a huge omnibus. The seats are generally comfortably stuffed and covered with velveteen, their backs being made to revolve on a pivot so that the passengers are enabled to place themselves either face to face or back to back to their next neighbors at their discretion.

Immediately after leaving Rochester the ticket-collector demanded the fare. I presented him with two bank notes. After examining one of them he exclaimed, " This is a forged bill." Forged or not, I replied, I received it from the last ticket-collector. Perceiving I was a stranger, he became more civil, but he refused the bill, so I tendered him another. Some of the railway conductors are particularly coarse-minded fellows and placed as they imagine, in some authority, they occasionally assume the manners of petty tyrants. It is scarcely possible to describe the style of contemptuous insolence with which they sometimes treat the passengers. However, in justice to the more refined States in the Northeastern portion of the Union, I am ready to testify that the unpleasant behavior to which I allude in no instance there occurred to me.

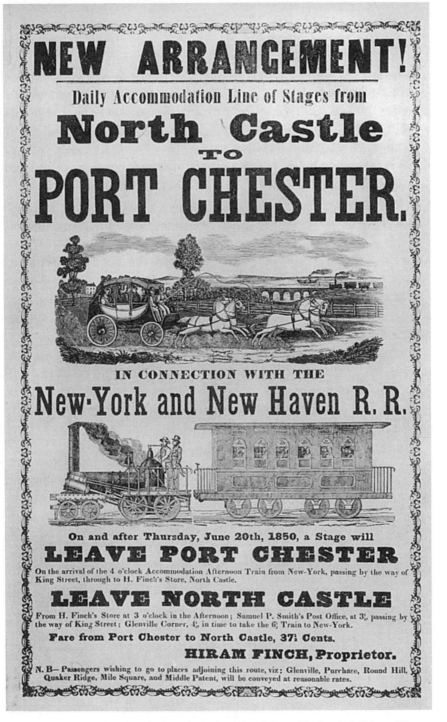

Advertisement for the New York and New Haven Railroad (by courtesy of the Columbia University Libraries)

The railway train on which I intended to return to Buffalo took its departure from the station at Niagara nearly a quarter of an hour before its proper time, leaving about forty of its passengers behind. From what we could learn, this appeared to be a trick arranged by some of the innkeepers to keep the travelers another day in their hotels, at least, so far from showing any regret or endeavoring to assist us in our predicament, they only laughed at us. After some persuasion the agent of the railroad agreed to put on an extra train.

We departed about one hour afterwards and had just proceeded half way when we felt a violent shock and the train stopped suddenly. On jumping out of the cars we discovered that the engine had run off the rails, that both itself and its tender were buried in the mud at the side of the road and that the baggage-car had also followed them some distance. I waited a considerable time, during which the engineer, assisted by many work people, made strenuous endeavors to put all to rights but without effect. Seeing a light wagon passing by, an American gentleman and myself agreed for a conveyance in that vehicle to the city of Buffalo.

One circumstance particularly struck me during my travels in the United States and that is that I scarcely ever saw a decrepit traveler or one suffering under severe physical infirmity. I observed, however, a number of florid fat travelers.

.   .   .   .   .   .

At dusk in the evening of November 8, I started from Macon for Savannah by railway. The evening was bitterly cold, but in consequence of an immense fire kept up in the stove in the car we were nearly suffocated with the heat. I observed the conductor constantly opening the door and looking out at the rear of the cars. I inquired the cause of his apparent uneasiness. He told me that frequent instances had happened of slaves escaping from the plantations and getting up behind the cars, and he added, " We have to be very particular now because we are held responsible for them by law should they escape in this manner."

We were detained upon the road longer than was usual in consequence of the difficulty of obtaining water for the engine. The country is sandy and dry, from which at some seasons great inconvenience resulted. After an unpleasant night journey we arrived at Savannah about seven o'clock on the morning of the 9th.

Our night's journey between Wilmington and Richmond on the railroad was far from agreeable. All chance of sleep was denied to us by reason of the frequent visits of the conductors, who at each small stopping-place constantly made a request to see our tickets, and also in consequence of our being obliged to change four different times from one set of cars into others. Once during the night we had to leave the train and pass through a town in an omnibus. These changes cause much personal inconvenience which by a little arrangement and agreement between the different companies might readily be avoided.

During my travels in the United States I was absent from Montreal fifty-three days, I traveled fifty-three hundred miles and my expenses were fifty-three pounds sterling.

◡◠ 1 8 5 3 ◠◡

THE RECOVERED DINNER

[From *Old England and New England*, Alfred Bunn (London, 1853), pp. 5, 279, 280, 281]

Now come we to the climacteric of traveling—the railroad cars. The cars are of an extraordinary length and width, capable of accommodating about fifty-six people, having on either side fourteen seats holding two people each. There is no room to deposit any small article under one's feet and even if there was they would be spit on to a certainty; indeed, even in the event of dropping money on the floor no decent person could venture to pick it up unless he put on an old glove.

The moment the cars start a string of filthy lads stream in offering for sale sweetmeats, apples, books and other important wares, and they are succeeded by travelers who, if they find no other accommodations, stand up in the middle of the cars and spit away. It is utterly impossible to mistake an American for anyone else. He has his feet on the

Advertisement for railroads between Philadelphia, Chicago, and St. Louis (by courtesy of the Columbia University Libraries)

seat next him, which he turns over for the purpose, or, if it is occupied, he sits with his knees " let in " to the back of it. He either sucks a piece of sweetmeat, bites a piece of wood or chews a bit of tobacco and invariably reads a newspaper.

In Summer they have blinds to the numerous windows on each side and in many trains they hand around tumblers of cold water, while in Winter there is a stove in each car plentifully supplied with fuel.

On reaching the dépôt you deposit your luggage with the baggage-master who fastens a check to each separate article, giving you a corresponding check, and all your effects will be safely delivered or in case of accident made good by the company. In America a small quantity of traveling equipage goes a long way. In Georgia, especially, the luggage considered essential for a journey of any distance consists of a shirt collar and a pair of spurs, and when I asked a native of that State how he managed about a shirt he said, " I can't spare the time to wait while they're cleaning it and if I could it's almost as cheap to buy a new one."

The occurrence of accidents is alarming in the highest degree and there can be no doubt of there being hundreds, the casualties of which have never been made known, it being deemed advisable not to agitate people's nerves to fever pitch. A friend of ours near whose country residence the Harlem Railroad runs invited a few friends to dine with him, bringing down a fine piece of roasting beef. When they quitted the cars, which had again got into motion, it was discovered that the beef had been forgotten and was almost out of sight.

" We shall lose our dinner after all," said a guest.

" No we shan't," said the host, " for the train generally meets with an accident about a mile further on and we shall get it again."

They ran on and sure enough an accident did happen. On coming up with the cars and ascertaining that the beef was in safety, without troubling themselves about the passengers, they recovered their meat and walked off with it.

THE WRECK EXPERT

[From *A Vacation Tour in the United States and Canada*, Charles Richard Weld (London, 1855), pp. 222, 225, 247]

On leaving Boston my destination was Saratoga, to which I traveled by railway, passing through the picturesque district of the Green Mountains. The American railway car is about forty feet long, eight and a half wide and six and a half high, having seats with reversible backs for sixty passengers. The weight of a car of these dimensions is eleven tons and the cost about $2,000. There are no porters at the stations. A conductor, unmarked by any badge of distinction beyond a small plate which he only displays when the train is in motion, shouts to the engine driver, " All o'board "; a bell attached to the engine is rung violently, not to summon indolent or tardy passengers, for they are supposed to be in the cars, but to warn people in the streets of the approach of the locomotive, and the train is off.

Thus the traveler has to look out for himself and he is early made aware of the important fact that if he trusts to others he will in all probability pay the penalty by being left behind. Through streets, across thronged roads speeds the train, the only warning being a conspicuous notice, Look Out For the Locomotive When the Bell Rings. The conductor's labors commence with the journey. As the functionary proceeds through the cars calling out " Tickets," it will be noticed that very few passengers are provided with them. The conductor is therefore empowered to sell tickets, and this, with receiving them at the end of the journey, constitutes his principal occupation. When the train reaches its destination the conductor removes his official badge and retires into private life.

The process of watering the passengers, as it is called, is another feature peculiar to American railway traveling. A man or boy, often a Negro, carrying a tin can and tumblers in a frame passes frequently through the cars dispensing iced water to the numerous applicants for that indispensable refreshment during an American Summer, which is provided at the expense of the railway company.

The rate of traveling is about twenty-four miles an hour. The stoppages are frequent to take in the wood, which burns rapidly. At these wooding-stations horses may be seen toiling up an endless incline, which retrogrades beneath their feet and sets machinery in motion which saws wood for the locomotives.

Following the left bank of the river, we arrived at Troy. The traveler has an excellent opportunity of seeing the streets as the railway passes directly through them, and passengers are conveniently dropped at the doors of the hotels.

.   .   .   .

It is a great convenience in America to' be enabled to take a through ticket for a long journey involving change of railways. In the present case Washington, 680 miles from Cincinnati, was my destination and although I had to travel over the lines belonging to different companies one ticket carried me through. Besides the saving of much trouble by this plan, it is a little less expensive.

I arrived in Cumberland on Saturday and proposed proceeding to Washington by a train due at Cumberland on Monday morning at eight o'clock and was in readiness with fourteen other passengers at the proper time. An hour having passed without any sign of the train, I inquired the cause of the delay, but as the telegraph was not in working order no certain answer could be given. It was surmised that an accident had happened and I was told that if the train did not arrive in another hour we should be sent by a special train.

Ten o'clock arrived but no train; accordingly three cars and a baggage-car were prepared for our conveyance. The first car was set apart for the colored portion of our party, consisting of three women and two men slaves. The second car was allotted to gentlemen and the third and last to ladies. As we were favored by the companionship of only four of the latter, no objection was made to all the gentlemen occupying seats with them. Thus the train was very light, the only heavy car being the baggage-car, which, besides our luggage, contained a large quantity of ice packed in sawdust.

As soon as we had taken our seats the bell rang and we dashed off. In a few minutes the conductor made his appearance and informed us that we were very late in starting and that it would take smart work to make up the time. To effect this required additional speed, which I had every reason to believe could not be maintained without serious danger. The conductor, however, was a determined man and as he evidently attached little value to his own life it was not to be expected that his passengers would be much cared for. The line after leaving Cumberland follows the windings of the Potomac, describing sharp curves. Round these the engine darted with rocket-like impetuosity, the car in which we were seated swaying in a manner rendering it necessary to hold on. A more significant hint of the impending catastrophe was given by the fall of a ponderous lamp glass on my head but with no worse result than inflicting a smart blow. Presently another glass was jerked out of its socket and precipitated into the lap of a lady; the oscillations of the car meanwhile increasing in violence.

Affairs now assumed a serious aspect and I felt certain we were on the eve of a smash. This was the opinion of a gentleman who had the care of two ladies, for he proceeded with a coolness deserving a better cause to instruct us how to place ourselves, laying great stress on the importance of sitting diagonally in order not to receive the shock directly on the knees. We were also advised to hold the backs of the seats before us. He strengthened his advice by assuring us that he was experienced in railway accidents and added that as there was far less danger in the middle than in the end car it would be prudent to change our seats at the next station.

As we expected, an accident did occur, the results of which, had we retained our seats in the last car, would have been in all probability most serious. In vain was the conductor urged to slacken the excessive speed. With blind if not wilful recklessness it was maintained and at length, when about six miles from the station where we changed our places, a terrific crash and a series of dislocatory heavings and collisions, terminating in deathlike silence and the overthrow of the car which we occupied, gave certain evidence that we had gone off the line.

I have no distinct recollection how I crawled out of the car, for I was half stunned, but I remember being highly delighted when I found my limbs sound. On looking around, the spectacle was extraordinary. With the exception of about half the middle car and engine there was scarcely a portion of the train that was not more or less broken. The

Collision of passenger and excursion trains near Camp Hill Station, Pennsylvania, July 17, 1856 (from *Frank Leslie's Illustrated Weekly*, July 26, 1856)

wheels were whirled to great distances and the rails for the length of many yards either wholly wrenched from the sleepers or converted into snakeheads.

When I saw the state of things I was extremely indignant, for by the wilful conduct of the conductor our lives had been placed in imminent peril, but when I spoke in strong terms of him to my fellow passengers, urging that we ought to report him to the directors of the line, I found my feelings were not only unshared but all rather approved than otherwise his exertions to get us in on time. Accidents on railways are thought so little of in America it is useless to remonstrate.

A camel-back engine was dispatched from the nearest station to remove our cars from the line, which they effectually blocked. This it
did in a very summary manner but when the line was clear we still
had to wait the arrival of the train from Baltimore, in cars detached
from which we were to be forwarded. At length, after a detention of
five hours, we resumed our journey and fortunately reached Harper's
Ferry without further accident.

ᲐᲛ 1 8 5 5 ᲐᲛ

THE BAGGAGE AGENT

[From *America by River and Rail*, William Ferguson (London,
1856), pp. 41, 108, 223, 233, 263]

We left Boston at half past two in the afternoon of March 6, 1855 by
what is called the Boston and New York Express Line, an arrangement
between four railways for running certain trains rapidly over their
roads direct from Boston to New York. In taking this route we pass
forty-four miles westward over the Boston and Worcester Railroad to
the town of Worcester; thence fifty-six miles over a portion of the
Western Railroad of Massachusetts to Springfield on the Connecticut
river. From Springfield the direction changes south for sixty-two miles
by the Hartford and New Haven Railroad till we reach New Haven,
and the remaining seventy-four miles is by the New York and New
Haven Railroad along the coast to New York. The whole distance is
two hundred and thirty-six miles, which was accomplished in nine
hours, and the fare was five dollars, a little over two cents a mile.

We became acquainted on this journey with some arrangements
which afterward were made very familiar and add much to the convenience of traveling. On arriving at the station of departure tickets
with a number and our destination were attached to each piece of baggage and a duplicate number given us. The baggage was then put in a
car and the traveler gives himself no more trouble about it. As the
end of the journey is approached a duly authorized baggage-agent

comes into the cars and receives your ticket, for which he gives his
receipt. You tell him your destination and he sees your baggage safely
delivered to your abode.

At Springfield the broad waters of the Connecticut river are spanned
by a long bridge from which we anticipated having a fine view, but
we were doomed to disappointment on this occasion and very often
afterward, for this bridge as well as others in America is roofed and
encased in wooden walls. These covered bridges are very ugly features of the landscape and the source of continual annoyance to the
tourist, who, just as he is straining to catch a glance up or down some
pretty stream finds himself whirled through a musty, close smelling,
dusty box.

The train stopped twenty minutes at Springfield for an early supper.
Bodily refreshment is never lost sight of in the arrangements of American traveling. Almost immediately after leaving Springfield night fell
and before long it was quite dark. The seats in the cars of this line are
the least disagreeable I met with in America; the backs are sufficiently
high to form an easy rest for the head and the footboard adjusts itself
to give your legs repose. The result of all this, especially after supper
and in the dark, which is only partially dispelled by the car lamps, is
that most people fell asleep, so the last part of the journey was quiet
enough.

In the outskirts of New York the locomotive leaves us. The rails
are laid in the middle of Fourth avenue and the Bowery to Canal street
and the locomotives are not permitted to pass through these. So at an
outer station the train was broken up and each car drawn into town
by horses with bells on their harness. Those who knew the city got
down in the street at the point nearest their destination.

We left the St. Nicholas Hotel, New York, in the morning, March
20, at half-past eight to go to Philadelphia by the New Jersey Railway.
Tickets are procured and baggage checked at a station on the New
York side of the Hudson river, over which we were ferried in a steamer
to New Jersey. Then we had to cross the open street to the regular
station of the company. We started from New Jersey a few minutes
past eight and reached Philadelphia, a distance of eighty-seven miles,
about twelve. We left Philadelphia the next day at noon, our destination being Charleston, S. C. and to reach it we traveled over eight

different railroads and went by water one part of the way. Our baggage we checked at Philadelphia to Washington so we had no more trouble with it until we got there and we got tickets to Wilmington, N. C.

These tickets are long contracts with seven coupons, one for each of the seven different links which, with the nominal one, make up this through route. We got to Baltimore on the Philadelphia, Wilmington and Baltimore Railroad about four, where change of cars number two took place. We were conveyed through the town in cars on a railway laid in the streets. I asked the conductor if the railroad had the prior right of passing over ordinary vehicles and he replied, " The city gives us the right of way through the streets and as to the right to pass first I take it and that's about how the law stands."

About five, they are not particular to a quarter of an hour, we left Baltimore on the Baltimore and Ohio Railroad and arrived at Washington just as it was getting dark. At Washington change number three takes place. We give up our baggage checks to the baggage-master of the new line, who looks after it for us. An omnibus of giant dimensions receives us and we are driven off through the city of Washington. It is a long way to the riverside and the houses seem few and far between. We have slowly descended a steep street to the Potomac and soon are on board the steamer.

First you get a check-ticket from the captain for your fare and pay for your supper if you mean to have any. Then comes the hunting up of your baggage and getting it checked, which is tedious enough. It is all piled up in the fore part of the boat. The baggage-master stands and cooly looks on, leaving you by the aid of a lantern to pick out your own trunks. This all over, we have leisure to make a good supper, enjoying especially some Potomac trout. Supper over, we get comfortably stretched on a couple of chairs and sleep until twelve, when we reach Acquia Creek and, changing for the fourth time, tumble half asleep into cars again and ride to Richmond on the Richmond, Fredericksburg and Potomac Railroad.

Somewhere about four or five in the morning we reach Richmond. It is very cold and we have to get out in the middle of the street in the snow, which has been falling while we were sleeping. Here we change for the fifth time and get into an omnibus to cross the town to another station. Before leaving, however, we have to amuse ourselves the best we can for more than half an hour. We fill it in by securing an early breakfast in a miserable eating-house attached to the station.

As daylight of the second morning was breaking we left Richmond on the Richmond and Petersburg Railroad for Petersburg. At Petersburg we have to change again a sixth time and ride more than two miles in an omnibus by a most up-hill and down-dale road. Seated once more in the cars, we find we must wait an hour before the train starts for Weldon, which it does at eight o'clock. The distance is sixty-four miles and we get there at eleven on the Petersburg Railroad and make the seventh change. This time both trains of cars are in the same

Stone Mountain, De Kalb County, Georgia (By courtesy of the Columbia University Libraries)

station. We dine here and at twelve o'clock are off again for Wilmington by the Weldon and Wilmington Railroad, a distance of one hundred and sixty-two miles, occupying eight hours. We traveled the whole distance through a forest of pines, unbroken save by some small settlement or resin gatherers' camp.

We might have gone on from Wilmington but we made change the eighth over night and slept at the Carolina House, a wretched enough place. We are called at half past five in the morning when we hurry down to the wharf, for the Cape Fear river has to be crossed before we get to the cars of the Wilmington and Manchester Railroad, by which we proceed south. The steamer plies in connection with the railroad and we get tickets for Charleston on board as well as our baggage re-checked. We reached the opposite bank and boarded the train and soon found ourselves proceeding through a swamp covered with a strange jungle of trees, shrubs and creepers. The railroad here, as through many other swamps, is built on a frame work supported by piles.

About eleven we were at a place called Fair Bluff, a clearing in the forest where the up and down trains meet, and stopped to dine. It was a forest dinner. Our host said he found great difficulty in procuring supplies, now that provisions are so scarce. The stations on this line are merely wooden houses or log huts, generally some turpentine dépôt. About five o'clock we reached Kingsville, the termination of this road. We had to wait nearly two hours here for a train on the Columbia branch of the South Carolina Railroad, so we had plenty of time for tea and to look around. There was nothing to see. It is a mere junction point in the midst of a swamp.

At last the train came up and proved to be a freight train, with one passenger car attached. By dint of the extremest packing the passengers all got in, but it was a horrible ride. The car was lower in the roof than usual, and narrower, and the seats were too small and too close together to sleep comfortably. After traveling so far the feeling of fatigue and pain in our bones became almost unbearable. Added to all there was a wood fire in the stove, which filled the air with irritating dryness, and as most of the male passengers were chewing tobacco there were many elements of discomfort. The distance to be traversed in these unhappy circumstances was one hundred and five miles and was got over at the rate of but little more than ten miles an hour. We arrived at Charleston on March 24 at four o'clock in the morning.

.   .   .   .   .   .

We left Philadelphia at half past seven on the morning of April 18 under the guidance of our friend the president of the Pennsylvania Railroad. The railway for seventy miles is very rough, so much so that the swinging and jolting, added to the hot air of the cars, gave me a feeling like seasickness. For a mile and a half from the station in Market street the train is drawn by horses. This portion of the road does not belong to the Pennsylvania Railroad. The first seventy miles is by the Columbia Railroad, which is owned by the State of Pennsylvania and connects Philadelphia with their canals. The country through which it passes is varied, well farmed and beautiful. At Dillerville, two miles beyond Lancaster we leave the state-owned road and proceed by the Lancaster and Harrisburg Railroad to Harrisburg. This road is much smoother.

We left Harrisburg at five o'clock in the afternoon by the fast train that had left Philadelphia at one, our destination for the night being Altoona at the foot of the mountains. It was quite dark before we reached Altoona and we were surprised and very glad to find a fine hotel there and repose in bedrooms which would do no discredit to Broadway. I awoke refreshed and sallied out at half past eight to see Altoona. The American telegraph, which was at work in the railroad office, may be said to both write and talk. It indents a long strip of paper with points and the young man who was attending it is so expert that he knows by listening to the click of the machine what is being telegraphed and can read by the sound. They were telegraphing from Pittsburgh, 117 miles distant, and it was wonderful to listen to a lad reading by ear the words that were being flashed such a distance.

The hotel had been perfectly still all the forenoon but for ten or fifteen minutes about one o'clock it became a scene of great bustle. The east and west trains meet for dinner. The long tables in the dining-hall stood in all order of great preparation one moment; the next they were overrun by the hungry passengers. In a few minutes provisions and people had alike disappeared and Altoona was once more left in quiet.

At Crestline we caught a train for Cleveland on the Cleveland, Columbus and Cincinnati Railroad and proceeded by it to Columbus. The soil on this section of the road is clay and in this dry weather the train raised a cloud of fine dust which was very disagreeable. The dust is a matter of such serious inconvenience on American railroads that it is no uncommon thing to see it put forth in the announcements of rival companies that certain roads are ballasted with broken stone or gravel as an inducement to travelers to prefer them on account of the less dust to which they are liable.

There was a convention of railway presidents and superintendents at the Neil House, where we took up our quarters. I was introduced to many of them and spent the forenoon in conversation with them at the offices of the Columbus and Xenia Railway Company. I may mention as a specimen of their generous hospitality that nearly everyone presented me with a free pass over the line of railway with which he happened to be connected.

∽ 1 8 5 7 ∾

A NIGHT TRIP TO WHEELING

[From *Life and Liberty in America*, Charles Mackay (New York, 1859), pp. 49, 50, 138]

November 3, 1857. At Rome, N. Y. an old man got into our car and did us the favor of remaining with us for upward of fifty miles of our journey. He plied during the whole of the time a vigorous trade in some quack medicine of his own concoction, which he declared to be good for fevers, agues, dyspepsias, rheumatisms and colics. The price was a dollar a bottle and among the sixty persons in our car he succeeded in getting no less than nine customers by dint of the most impudent and vexatious pertinacity I ever beheld. Having exhausted our car, the peddler disappeared into the car adjoining, where he no doubt carried on the same performance.

We were no sooner relieved of his presence when a book hawker made his appearance and left a prospectus with every traveler to study or cast on the floor, and after a sufficient interval returned for orders. But the book trade did not appear to be very prosperous and he gathered up his prospectuses to do service on a future occasion. Then, changing his literary business for that of a dealer in maple candy, peppermint drops, cakes and apples, he allowed us no cessation from importunity until we arrived at the city of Rochester, where a new set of plagues of the same kind took possession of us and accompanied us the whole way to Niagara.

.   .   .   .   .   .

After traveling all night from Cumberland, Md., we arrived at the little dingy, dull city of Wheeling in Western Virginia before daylight, and hastened to our beds to snatch the sleep which is next to impossible to win or even to woo in the hot, frowsy, uncomfortable railway car, containing from fifty to sixty people and a demoniacal furnace burning anthracite coal. Without a proper place to stow away one's hat, with no convenience even to repose the head or back except to the ordinary height of a chair, with a current of cold air continually streaming in and rendered necessary by the sulphurous heat of the furnace, and with the constant slamming of the doors at either end of the car as the conductor goes in or out, or some weary passenger steps onto the platform to have a smoke, the passenger must indeed be dead beat who can sleep or even doze in a railroad car.

.   .   .   .   .   .

January, 1858. After no less than four accidents to our train on the Ohio and Mississippi Railroad, happily involving no other evil consequences than the smashing of the engine and two or three cars, the sacrifice of many valuable hours and the loss of an amount of patience difficult to estimate, we arrived at the miserable village, though called a city, of Jeffersonville, Indiana, nearly opposite Louisville, Kentucky. The train was due at an early hour of the afternoon but did not reach Jeffersonville until half past nine in the evening, long after the steam ferry boat had ceased to ply, and the captain of which refused to relight the fires of his boilers to carry the passengers across. We had had nothing to eat or drink all day in consequence of the accident to our

Advertisement for The Adams Express Company (By courtesy of the Columbia University Libraries)

train having befallen us in an out of the way place and in the very heart of the wilderness. We looked forward to a comfortable supper and a glass of wine or toddy after our fatigue and disappointments. There being no means of crossing the river, we were all reluctantly compelled to betake ourselves to the best inn in Jeffersonville, and bad, very bad, was the best.

Leaving Jeffersonville three days later, after visiting Louisville, we had not proceeded five hundred yards from the station when our locomotive, which happily had not put on all its steam, ran off the rails and stuck hard and dry upon the embankment. Here we waited two hours in hope of assistance, but nothing being forthcoming, we made the best of the calamity and returned to our old quarters in Louisville for another day.

AN EARLY AIR-CONDITIONED CAR

[From *Forty Years of American Life 1821–1861*, Thomas Low
Nichols, M. D. (London, 1864), pp. 241, 242]

The cars, as the Americans designate their railway carriages, on the road
from Cleveland to Cincinnati, were among the nicest I have ever seen.
They were not only brightly painted, gilded, upholstered and furnished
with retiring-rooms, but are warmed in Winter, cooled in Summer and
thoroughly ventilated always. In the warmest days of an American
Summer, with the thermometer at a hundred and the train enveloped in
clouds of dust, these cars are clean, airy and cool. By ingenious machinery a constant current of air is cooled and washed clean from dust
by being made to pass through showers of water. In Winter these cars
are warmed and ventilated with hot air supplied in great abundance by
suitable apparatus. They seat fifty or sixty passengers. The gentlemanly
conductor walks through the entire train to examine tickets when it is
in rapid motion: so the boy who sells newspapers, books and sugar-
plums has free access and the colored gentleman who supplies the
passengers with water where that luxury is not kept in well-iced
reservoirs in every car.

From Cincinnati we took the Western road for Cairo. Forests dark
and dreary, newly cleared farms and newly built villages are the monotonous accompaniments of a Western journey. The railroad itself is
tiresome in its straight lined and dead level uniformity. The only variety
we had was that of the violent motion caused by the displacement of
the ties by the frost. This was so great at times as to set all the cars
dancing and almost throw the passengers from their seats.

Advertisement for the Newburyport Railroad (by courtesy of the Columbia University Libraries)

GREELEY ON SLEEPING CARS

[From *An Overland Journey from New York to San Francisco*,
Horace Greeley (New York, 1860), pp. 7, 8]

I left New York by the Erie Railroad on Monday evening, May 9. Two hours later the gathered clouds burst upon us in a rain which continued through the night. We had glimpses of sunshine as we skirted the shore of Lake Erie on Wednesday and some more after a heavy shower at Chicago on Thursday.

Coming up the Erie I tried a sleeping-car for the third time and not very successfully. We all retired at ten o'clock with a fair allowance of open windows and virtuous resolutions, but the rain poured, the night was chill and damp, and soon every orifice for the admission of external air, save the two or three humbug ventilators overhead, was shut and a mephitic atmosphere produced. After gasping awhile like a netted fish on a hot sandbank I rose to enter my solemn protest against all sleeping-cars not provided with abundant and indefeasible means of ventilation. I tried one two nights later on the Michigan Southern Road (Woodruff car) which served much better but still far from perfect. It is very true that no arrangement can secure a healthy circulation of air by night in any passenger-car while the popular ignorance is so dense that the great majority imagine any atmosphere healthy that is neither too cold nor too hot, but the builders of cars have no right to be ignorant of the laws of life with which they tamper and two or three presentments by grand juries of the makers of unventilated cars, especially sleeping-cars, as guilty of manslaughter would exert a most salutary influence. I commend this public duty to the immediate consideration of jurors and prosecutors.

Stopping at Hornellsville at seven next morning, I took the train for Buffalo at noon and halted at Castile to fulfill an engagement to speak at Pike. I left Pike for Castile at five on Wednesday morning; took the cars to Buffalo at half-past seven, was in ample time for the Lake Shore train at ten, ran into Cleveland a little after five, left at six for

Toledo, where we changed cars between ten and eleven, and were in Chicago at seven next morning.

.   .   .   .   .   .

The *Pike* rounded to at Hannibal and sent us ashore. The train backed down to within forty feet of her and the passengers got aboard followed by their baggage, and in half an hour we were steaming up through the wooded ravine to emerge on one of the largest prairies in northern Missouri. Across this or rather along it we took our course westward almost as the crow flies to St. Joseph on the Missouri, two hundred and six miles distant, which we reached in a little more than twelve hours. The road was completed in hot haste last Winter in order to profit by the Pike's Peak migration this Spring. No gravel is to be found on its

Smith's reclining car seat, 1856 (from the *American Railroad Journal*, January, 1856)

line and as it was raining pitilessly for the second day the roadbed was a causeway of mortar or ooze into which the passing train pressed the ties, first on one side, then on the other making the track as bad as track could well be. A year hence it must be better even with the frost coming out of the ground, or after a dry week it probably will be quite fair, but yesterday it afforded more exercise to the mile than any other railroad I have ever traveled on.

This road was run so as to avoid the more settled districts and thus to secure a larger allotment of the public lands but I had not believed it possible to run a railroad through northern Missouri so as to strike so few settlements.

ᜒ 1 8 6 0 ᜒ

THE WAGNER SLEEPING CAR

[From *Criss-Cross Journeys*, Walter Thornbury (London, 1873), pp. 25-31]

I traveled in the *Lightning Express* from Nashville to Memphis in the Autumn of 1860. The line is a good safe line but not an air line, as the Americans call those of their railroads that run across level prairies, as in Indiana and Wisconsin, without curves or grades. The cars are of the Russian sledge-body model and contain from forty to fifty passengers. The seats, holding two persons each, are ranged in rows down each side of the car, with a path for the conductor and itinerant salesmen down the middle. The seats have low backs which are sometimes padded with velvet or on the poorer lines with carpet or leather. The floors are always carpeted or matted and the windows generally have Venetian blinds and shutters for the night or for the severe cold weather. There is always at one end of each car a large stone filter with a tin cup attached. On most lines, especially in the South, a Negro boy or girl comes around every half hour and offers a glass of water from the cool, gurgling jug.

The conductor wears no uniform except a cap with a band labelled

Night Travel on the New York Central in 1858 (from
Harper's Illustrated Weekly, October 2, 1858)

Conductor. He works in and out through the doors at either end that lead from one car to another and this perpetual slamming of the fore door and aft door is a special irritation, particularly when one wants to get to sleep. He appears at every station to examine the tickets of the newcomers and to give them in exchange a check with a list of stations and distances on the back. The brakeman, sometimes a great laughing Negro in the far South, stands outside the car door on the platform where men go to smoke or meditatively expectorate as they watch the half-cleared forests through which we tear. This is not the smokers' special stand and perch as there is always a smoking-car to every train and a ladies' car where no smoking is allowed. The smoking-car is small, with seats running all around, and there is a table in the middle on which the newsboy generally spreads his store of intellectual sophistry. It is the den from which he emerges to deliver his five-cent oracles.

No want can arise in the traveler's mind that there is not some one in the train ready to administer to. Every town you pass pelts you with its daily papers. If you stop for ten minutes at a central station a quack is sure to come into the car and inform everyone that the Dead Shot Worm Candy is now selling at twenty-five cents the packet, that Vestris's Bloom, the finest cosmetic in the known world, is to be had for a half dollar the quarter pound, or that Knickerbocker's Corn Exterminator makes life's path easy at a dime the ounce packet. Presently you fall asleep and awaken covered with a heavy snow of handbills about Harper's reprints and Peterson's unscrupulous robberies from English authors. Anon, a huge fellow with enormous apples, two cents each, peaches in their season, hickory nuts, pecans or maple sugar cakes. To them succeed sellers of ivory combs, parched corn and packets of mixed sweetmeats.

I do not touch on the sanitary arrangements of the cars, which are excellent, but I must remark on the truly admirable system by which the conductor or even the passengers can in case of fire or murderous assault or other necessity at once communicate with the engine driver and instantly stop the train. It consists of a cord running in loops along the roof of every carriage and attached at one end to a bell or dial on the engine.

I was going from Albany to Buffalo. The conductor seeing me walking about the platform and eyeing the several cars said to me with sagacious forethought, "Sleeping-car, mister? Going through, stranger?" I replied that I was and followed the man into the last car, which was lettered in large letters on a sunflower ground, Albany and Buffalo Sleeping-Car. I entered and found that it was like the ordinary railway-car with the usual filter and stove and with the seats arranged in the usual manner. I asked how much extra I must pay for a bed. "Single high, twenty-five cents, double low, half a dollar," said the officer on duty. I ordered a single high and as I paid my twenty-five cents the bell on the engine began to get restless. Ten other persons entered and ordered beds and paid for them with more or less complaint and wrangling.

When we were between Little Falls and Herkeimer the officer of the sleeping-car entered and called out, "Now then, misters, if you please, get up from your seats and allow me to make up the beds." Two by two we arose and with quick hand the nimble Yankee turned over every other seat so as to reverse the back and make two seats facing each other. He shut the windows and pulled up the shutters, leaving for ventilation the slip of perforated zinc open at the top of each. Then he stripped up the cushions and unfastened from beneath each seat a light cane-bottomed frame which he fastened to the side of the car at suitable heights and covered each with cushions and blankets.

I went out on the balcony to be out of the way and when I came back the whole place was transformed. There was no longer an aisle of double seats but the cabin of a small steamer with curtained berths and closed portholes. The bottom berths were wide and comfortable with room to roll and turn. There were two high berths to choose from; both wicker trays, ledged in, cushioned and rugged. The one was about a foot and a half higher than the other and I choose the top one as being nearer the zinc ventilator. Some of the passengers had turned in and were snoring. Others, like young cows balancing on spring boughs, were swinging their legs from the wicker trays and peeling off their stockings or struggling to get rid of their boots.

I clambered to my perch and found it was like lying on one's back on a narrow plank. If I turned my back to the car wall the motion of the train bumped me off my bed altogether and if I turned my face to the

Interior of a Wagner sleeping car on the New York Central, 1859 (from *Frank Leslie's Illustrated Weekly*, April, 1859)

wall I felt a horrible sensation of being likely to roll backward into the aisle, so I lay on my back and settled the question. It was like trying to sleep on the back of a runaway horse. At each place the train stopped there was the clashing of the bell and if I peered through the zinc ventilator into the outer darkness a flying scud of sparks from the engine did not serve to divest my mind of all chances of being burnt alive. Then there were blazes of pine torches as we neared a station, more bell clamor and jumbling sounds of baggage, slamming doors and itinerant conductors.

At last I fell into a precarious and fragile sleep that lasted until daylight returned. One by one the passengers woke up, yawned, and stretched themselves. There was something suspicious in the haste in

Interior of a Wagner sleeping car, 1897 (by courtesy
of the *Railroad Age*)

which we all flopped out of bed, for no really comfortable bed was ever left with such coarse ingratitude. Presently the attendant entered and proceeded to readjust the seats, and through the opened windows there came a draft of pure air that freshened our frowsy and dishevelled crew. We repaired to the washing-room which contained one dirty brush fastened to the wall by a chain and a basin. There was very little water and the basin had to be tilted to one side to get enough for even a scanty rinsing.

By this time we were near Buffalo and breakfast. The train slackened and stopped and out poured the hungry swarms. Five gongs of five opposition breakfast places banged and thundered for our custom. In a minute I was seated with some thirty other hungry souls stowing away white piles of hominy, pink shavings of corned beef and bowls of stewed oysters, while a Negro boy waved a plume brush of wild turkey feathers over my head to keep off the greedy flies.

~ 1 8 6 4 ~

THE RAILWAY ACCIDENT GAZETTE

[From *America During and After the War*, Robert Ferguson (London, 1866), pp. 18, 19, 60, 61]

In America the railroad seems to be considered a public highway on which the company has the right of toll. When you enter a station you see no porters from whom to make an inquiry, nor is there any person whose business it is to find you a seat. There is no one to examine your ticket to see that you are all right before you start, and no one whose duty it is to prevent you from breaking your neck by getting in when the train is in motion. You must find out your train and take your place as best you can. The conductor usually cries " All aboard! " when the train is about to start, but sometimes when it is ready it silently moves off.

At Albany we changed trains for Niagara and I made my first acquaintance with the sleeping-car. The sleeping-car is in the day time like any other car but by a number of ingenious contrivances its transformation is effected in a very short time, as when the train stops for supper. Each pair of seats makes up into one bed, so that a person when lying takes up just the same room as four persons sitting. Then, by means of various supports and appliances attached to the sides of the car, a second tier of beds is arranged above the first. Sometimes there is a third tier but this is not the general rule and crowds the car to an uncomfortable extent. In some cases there are berths completely partitioned off, so that ladies may regularly go to bed if they like in all privacy. At each end there is generally a stove and also a place for washing in the morning.

Travelers have sometimes complained of unpleasant closeness in these cars but inasmuch as they generally contain only one half and in no case more than three-fourths of the ordinary number of passengers and as the means of ventilation are at least equal to those in the other cars it is evident that this is not an essential condition of the sleeping-cars. These cars are not generally run by the railroad companies themselves but are the property of private individuals or of companies. You pay your ordinary fare to the railroad company and when you get into the sleeping-car you pay the additional charge, generally not more than fifty cents, to the person appointed to receive it.

The most uncomfortable part of the proceedings I found to be getting up in the morning, while the car was being transformed into its former state, and the occupants were crowded into the narrow passageway in the middle.

.   .   .   .   .   .

We started from Washington by steamer for Richmond by way of Acquia Creek. It was a lovely morning and the passengers were scattered about smoking, reading or playing euchre when a person came around with a sheaf of newspapers which he began to distribute. Judge of my surprise when I found it to be what might be called the *Railway Accident Gazette*, in fact a record of the principal accidents that had happened in the United States in the last six months. All the most frightful cases of smashing to pieces, scalding to death, drownings, blowing up into the air were arrayed before the eyes of the dismayed traveler. I was at a loss to conceive the meaning of the cold-blooded cruelty of giving the unfortunate passengers such a record. This, however, was presently explained by the return of our tormentor bring with him a note book and a bundle of tickets and I found that he was the agent of a Life Insurance Company whose business it was, first to terrify the passengers into a suitable frame of mind, and then to insure their lives for them.

⌒ 1 8 6 7 ⌒

WHEN PASSENGERS WENT ARMED

[From *Last Winter in the United States*, F. Barham Zincke (London, 1868), pp. 110, 111, 127, 148, 149]

American ladies, having been well broken into the publicity of their system of railway traveling, make the best of it and seem quite unconcerned about what would appear to those unused to it its disagreeable features. Never but with one exception did I pass a night on the railroad without finding a sleeping-car attached to the train. It was in the South and there happened to be about forty people in the car, of which eight or ten were married ladies traveling with their husbands, and, like everybody one sees in America, they were young and of course better looking than the generality of the fair sex. English ladies would probably under circumstances of so much publicity have endeavored to keep awake but their American sisters passed the night as comfortably as might be, each laying her head on her husband's shoulder for a pillow. In the morning, when the train stopped an hour for breakfast, they made their toilette in the car, there being generally an abundance of water in a railway-car with a mug to drink from and a basin to wash in. They appeared all to have with them brushes and combs and towels and soap.

In the South there is not the same value set on time as in the North. I often saw trains stopped, not at a station, for the purpose of taking up or setting down a single passenger. I even saw this done that a parcel or letter might be taken from a person standing by the railway side. On one occasion an acquaintance with whom I was traveling that day and myself both happened to have had no dinner. We mentioned this to the conductor and asked him if he could manage in any way to let us have some supper. "Oh yes," he readily replied, "I will at eleven o'clock stop the train at a house in the forest where I sometimes have supper myself. I will give you twenty minutes." I suppose the other passengers, none of whom left their seats, imagined that we had stopped to repair some small damage or to take in wood or water, for on returing to the car we heard no observations made on the delay.

The railroad cow-catcher, which we used to see frequently mentioned in books on American travel appears now to have been superseded by another contrivance with a different form, for in the United States nothing remains long in one form. The new form resembles that of the snow-plow and it must act by partially lifting what it comes into contact with and then throwing it off to the right or left. This cow-plough does not always do its work. Not far from the town of Jackson, Miss., we came up with one of these poor animals that happened to be lying on the rails. On this occasion the plough went over it and so did the first two or three cars till at last the unhappy brute got fast fixed among the springs and wheels of the car I was in.

The train was stopped and the cow taken out, which, though horribly mangled proved to be still alive. The conductor called out for the loan of a pistol to enable him to put it out of its misery. In an instant almost from every window on that side of the train a hand was extended offering the desired instrument. On my making some observations on the number of pistols that were forthcoming ready-loaded at a moment's notice, the gentleman seated next to me replied that it was quite possible that I was the only man unarmed on the train; in consequence of the frequent robberies no one ever thought of moving without his six-shooter.

Wagner drawing-room car, 1866 (by courtesy of the New York Central System)

THE WAGNER DRAWING-ROOM CAR

[From *Sketches of the South and West*, Henry Deedes (Edinburgh, 1869), pp. 68, 69, 79, 80, 160, 161]

At Louisville I took tickets for Jackson, Miss., but unfortunately had my luggage, some portion of which afterward came to grief, checked only to Humboldt, intending to lay over there and then take the train direct to Jackson. I had a strong desire, however, to see Memphis and was induced by the persuasive eloquence of the conductor to alter my plans; so I passed the roadside station of Humboldt which certainly did not look inviting, had our luggage re-checked and made ourselves comfortable for the night in the sleeping-car. The conductor was an Irishman and loud in accusations against England. There was, I think, only one other occupant of the sleeping-car and he also was going to Jackson. The night was fine and clear and nothing worthy of remark occurring we reached Memphis about 9 A.M. after twenty-three hours' travel. Some hours before arriving at Memphis we passed over a marvelous wooden bridge and piece of trellis-work extending upward of a mile and as I stood on the platform with my friend the conductor and felt the vibration of the rails and timbers I certainly did feel rather glad I had not to return that way.

For the information of those of my readers who have not experienced the luxury of a sleeping-car I will endeavor to describe the article. The car during the day is not different from the others unless perhaps it may be a little higher and therefore better ventilated. The seats are all ranged one behind another, but the backs, by an ingenious contrivance, are reversible, so the two seats can when required be made to face one another.

About nine o'clock the attendant comes to make up the beds. He turns the seat the way I have described, draws out an under seat till the two meet and letting down a flap from the side of the car forms another berth. Another above this one produces mattresses, pillows, sheets, blankets and wadded quilts and in a brace of shakes a bed or rather four beds are ready. There is a partition at the head and foot and curtains in front to render the whole as private as such a place can be made. To the south of the Ohio river the gentlemen's portion of the car is divided by a curtain from the remainder, which is appropriated to the ladies or to couples, and a separate dressing-room is provided at each end. In the North this luxury is dispensed with and ladies have to take their turn with the lords of creation.

During the night we had to stop and change cars and either then or whilst indulging in such sleep as the cars permitted I was relieved of my purse, and when I opened my bag, which was locked, I discovered the sides had been forced open and sundry most useful articles abstracted. Of course no redress could be obtained. Had I lost my bag and kept my check I could have claimed damages but as the line we traveled over belonged to two or three companies each said it could not have happened on their line and I had to put up with the loss the best I could. So much for the system of checks and baggage-masters.

.   .   .   .   .   .

The fare from Chicago to New York was forty dollars for two persons and an additional sum of sixteen dollars secured us a private compartment throughout the journey, or twenty-eight dollars each for a journey of upwards of 900 miles and 40 hours of time. At Rochester the line runs into the New York Central and you change into a [Wagner] drawing-room car, this being a day service of seventeen hours. The carriages are divided into compartments for four, eight and twelve, two dollars additional, which is included in the sixteen dollars I have mentioned, being charged for each reserved seat. For instance, we, being two in number, took four places and had a sort of box to ourselves for that portion of the journey.

∽ 1 8 6 8 ∾

INDIANS

[From *The Pacific Tourist*, Henry T. Williams (New York, 1876), p. 36]

In September 1868 a band of Sioux attempted to destroy a train between Alkali and Ogalalla. They lifted the rails from their chairs on the ties—raising only one end of each rail—about three feet, piling ties under them for support and firmly lashing the rails and ties together with wire from the adjoining telegraph line. They were pretty cunning in this arrangement of the rails and evidently placed them where they thought they would penetrate the cylinders on both sides of the engine. It was a straight track and as the train came up the cylinders were penetrated as they planned, the engine going over into the ditch with the cars piled up on top of it. The engineer and one of the brakemen who was on the engine at the time were thrown through the window of the cab and were little hurt. The fireman was fastened against the end of the boiler by the tender and the poor fellow was literally roasted to death.

All the trains at this time carried arms, and the conductor, with two or three passengers, among them, Father Ryan, a Catholic priest of Columbus, Nebraska, seized the arms and defended the train. The Indians meanwhile sulked among the bluffs near the track and occasionally fired a shot. Word was sent to North Platte and an engine and men came up who cleared the track. Meanwhile word was sent to Major North, then at Willow Island, to take one company of his

Pawnee scouts and follow the Indians. He came to Alkali and reported to Colonel Mizner, who was marching from North Platte with two companies of cavalry, all of whom started in pursuit. They went over to the North Platte River, crossed that stream and entered the sandhills where the scouts overtook and killed two of the Indians.

That night some of the white soldiers let their camp fire get away into the prairie and an immense prairie fire was the result. This, of course, alarmed the Indians and further pursuit was abandoned, much to the disgust of the scouts. Colonel Mizner also claimed that his rations were running short, but from all the facts we can learn he lacked the disposition to pursue and capture those Indians. The Indians have made some efforts to ditch a few trains since that year but have effected no serious damage.

Passenger train attacked by Indians near Cheyenne, June 14, 1870 (from *Frank Leslie's Illustrated Weekly*, July 9, 1870)

A BARBECUE NEAR ELKO

[From *Westward by Rail*, W. F. Rae (London, 1870), pp. 23, 28, 29, 30, 53, 76, 77]

Before beginning my journey by rail in September, 1869, from the Atlantic coast to the Pacific slope, I had to ascertain various particulars as to the route. There was no difficulty in purchasing a through ticket. In most of the hotels and in numerous shops the tickets of any railroad in the United States can be bought. The traveler sees innumerable advertisements in which the Union Pacific Railroad is conspicuous but in which the names of various lines are enumerated as being in connection with it. He reads in one that the Allentown Line is the shortest and best, in another that the Great Central Route is without a rival, or he may see the advantages of the Erie extolled to the skies. As the fare in all cases is the same the puzzle consists in ascertaining the respective merits of the competing lines. He learns that in any event he must first reach Chicago. If he is curious to become acquainted with the far famed Pullman cars he will decide to travel by the Great Central Route and that is the one I chose.

The traveler bound for the Far West starts from New York in the evening by the Pacific Express and on the morning of the following day arrives at Rochester where Pullman palace-cars are attached to the train. I had heard much said in praise of the Pullman car but I was unprepared for the reality. The first trip in one of these cars forms an epoch in a traveler's life. No royal personage can be more comfortably housed than the occupant of a Pullman car, provided the car be a hotel one. In the train by which I traveled one out of three sleeping-cars was of the latter description.

The hotel-car is divided into sections forming staterooms wherein parties of four can be accommodated. Between these rooms are seats arranged in the usual way. At the rear is a kitchen, which, though small, contains every appliance necessary for cooking purposes. There are water-tanks in which is stored a supply of water for washing and drinking sufficient to last the journey. A wine cellar contains the liquors which are likely to be in demand and an icehouse preserves ice for the gratification of those who prefer cold beverages. At stated intervals the conductor walks around taking passengers' orders, who make their selections from the bill-of-fare.

The choice is by no means small. Five different kinds of bread, four sorts of cold meat, six hot dishes, to say nothing of eggs cooked in seven different ways and all the seasonable vegetables and fruits, form a variety from which the most dainty eater might easily find something to tickle his palate and the ravenous to satisfy his appetite. The meal is served on a table temporarily fixed to the side of the car and removed when no longer required. To breakfast, dine and sup in this style while the train is speeding at the rate of nearly thirty miles an hour is a sensation of which the novelty is not greater than the comfort An additional zest is given to the good things by the thought that the passengers in the other cars must rush out when the refreshment station is reached and hastily swallow an ill-cooked meal.

The lines of railroad over which this train runs are the Hudson River, the New York Central, the Great Western of Canada and the Michigan Central. After passing two nights and one day in the railway car I arrived at Chicago.

If the Michigan Central express-train arrives punctually at Chicago there is no difficulty in continuing the journey toward the Pacific. Seventy-five minutes are allowed for getting from the station of arrival to the station of departure. In my own case the times of the trains did not correspond; the one train had started an hour before the other arrived. This is not the only illustration in my experience of the want of punctuality on the part of the railroad companies. My fellow passengers took the disappointment very quietly, regarding the short-coming as a matter of course. This failure involved a delay of twenty-four hours as there is but one through-train daily over the Pacific line. As I had intended to make a brief sojourn in Chicago I was even more unconcerned than my philosophical fellow travelers.

One through-train a day leaves Chicago for the Pacific Coast. The advertisements announce the starting of two trains but the traveler who starts by the evening train finds that he must spend a night in Omaha.

I purchased a ticket by the Chicago and Northwestern Railway and arrived at the station in time to get my baggage checked and then took my place in a Pullman palace-car at 10:15 in the morning. There was great bustle and confusion at the station as there are no porters and each passenger must look out for himself. If he is experienced he will have no more baggage than he can move unassisted.

When the moment for departure arrived the conductor called out "All aboard!," the engine gave a low and not unmelodious whistle, and the train started for the journey across the prairie. Five hours after leaving Chicago it reached the bridge which crosses the Mississippi. This bridge is nearly a mile in length and is constructed partly of wood and partly of iron. The structure has a very unsubstantial appearance and as it creaks and sways as the train passes over it the contingency of a descent into the rapid stream below passes over the mind.

On arriving at Council Bluffs we found omnibuses in waiting at the station but only a small proportion of the passengers could get inside seats, the remainder having the option of either sitting on the roof among the baggage or being left behind. In itself the seat on the roof was not objectionable, provided the time was short, but nearly an hour was required to make the trip to the station in Omaha. At the station confusion reigned supreme as at most American railway stations. Excited passengers were rushing about in quest of the baggage which, despite the system of checking, is often going astray or getting out of sight. Frantic efforts were made to attract the attention of the baggage-clerk and induce him to attach the necessary checks to the trunk or portmanteau which had at length been discovered.

Those who got this part of their business over proceeded to the office to secure berths in the Pullman sleepers. The number of these berths is limited and bitter was the disappointment of those who failed in obtaining one. The prospect of spending several nights in an ordinary car is enough to depress the mind and daunt the courage of the hardiest traveler. Having had the good fortune to be among those who had secured berths by telegraph, I was able to hear the exclamations of the disappointed with pleasant equanimity. As a class, the passengers differed greatly from those with whom I journeyed to Omaha from Chicago. A considerable proportion consisted of adventurers bound to

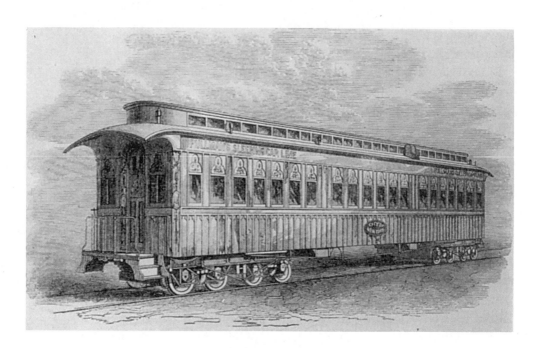

Pullman sleeping car, 1869 (from the *Illustrated London News*, October, 1869)

California to seek their fortune and a very few were traveling for their pleasure. To nearly every one the journey is a new one partaking of the character of a daring enterprise.

Four miles from Omaha the first stop is made. The journey is now fairly begun and everyone is on the lookout for new scenery and strange adventures. The first real sensation is obtained at Jackson, a small station a hundred miles from Omaha. Here many of the passengers see genuine Indians for the first time. They are Pawnees and we are told that they are friendly Indians, being supported by the United States Government. They may be friendly at heart but they are bloodthirsty in appearance. At Grand Island station the train stops and the passengers are allowed a half hour for supper. On leaving this place the traveler is told that if of a religious turn of mind he may bid good-bye to schools and churches and keep his eye peeled for buffalo. The event of the succeeding morning was halting at Cheyenne for breakfast, which was a plain but wholesome meal and had the charm of novelty in the shape of antelope steaks.

Promontory is the western terminus of the Union Pacific and the eastern terminus of the Central Pacific. At this point passengers have to change cars, secure fresh sleeping-berths and get their baggage moved from one train to the other. Two hours are allowed for this, as well as for taking a meal. Pullman palace-cars do not form a part of the ordinary trains on the Central Pacific Railway. The company has what it calls silver palace-cars, of which the name is the best part. They are very inferior when compared to those of the Pullman Company. Besides, the system of management is far less perfect. In the Pullman cars there is a conductor whose duty it is to see that the passengers are properly cared for and under him are colored servants, one being attached to each car. The Central Pacific cars are in charge of a colored man who also acts as attendant and this double duty is generally done badly.

The morning after leaving Elko there was a commotion among the passengers. A sudden shock roused all from their slumbers and while many were greatly frightened no one was seriously hurt. The engine and tender had been thrown off the rails in a collision with a herd of cattle and two oxen had been crushed to death. As it was, a detention of eight hours and the loss of breakfast were the only sufferings to be borne, and some of the passengers were indisposed to forego their breakfasts without an effort to provide a substitute. There was plenty of beef along side the line and the sage brush could be used for fuel. The sage brush was soon in a blaze but the meat could not be procured with equal rapidity. Cutting through an ox hide and carving out a steak with a penknife was a task that baffled the passenger who made the attempt.

Eight hours after the collision had occurred the engine was replaced on the rails and the train was put in motion again. The engine driver ran extra risks to make up the time lost and the descent from Summit Station to Sacramento was made with exceptional rapidity. The velocity with which the train rushed down this incline and the suddenness with which it wheeled around the curves produced a sensation which cannot be reproduced in words. The axle boxes smoked with friction and the odor of burning wood pervaded the cars. The wheels were nearly red-hot and in the darkness of the night they resembled discs of flame. Glad though all were to reach Sacramento, not a few were especially thankful to have reached it with whole limbs and unbruised bodies.

Baltimore & Ohio coach, 1863 (by courtesy of the Baltimore & Ohio Railroad)

ᥕᥕ 1 8 7 1 ᥕᥕ

THE PULLMAN HOTEL CAR

[From *Across the Ferry*, James Macaulay (London, 1887), pp. 137, 138]

The average speed on the American lines is about twenty miles an hour. The express trains rarely exceed thirty miles. Nominally, there is but one class of passengers and one scale of fare. Every traveler takes his place where he has a fancy except that there is a car reserved for ladies and for gentlemen accompanying them. But though in theory all are equal there are practically various classes of passengers. On the main lines there are cheap trains for immigrants. There are attached to most trains drawing-room cars, reclining-chair cars and sleeping-cars, for which additional charge is made. Some of these select cars belong to speculating builders or companies who purchase the privilege of attaching them to the trains and make their profit by the additional charge.

The most notable of these speculations are the Pullman hotel-cars. In one of these I traveled from Niagara to Chicago, leaving in the forenoon and arriving on the morning of the following day. Two of us chartered a compartment like the cabin of a ship with a comfortable

Interior of a palace hotel car on the Union Pacific, 1869 (from *Harper's Illustrated Weekly*, May, 1869)

sota above which a board was fixed at night, so as to form a second sleeping-berth. The beds were regularly made, boots put outside the door for cleaning, and hot water brought in the morning by an active black boy. Meals were served on a table carried into the cabin. The bill-of-fare contained many items and at moderate charges. For lamb chop or mutton chop and tomato sauce the price was seventy-five cents; fresh mackerel, fifty cents; omelet with ham, forty cents and a spring chicken cost a dollar. There was ample choice of vegetables, fruit and relishes with five or six kinds of wine in the *carte*. A cup of French coffee, tea or chocolate was fifteen cents. The kitchen, clean and commodious, had every appliance for cooking, and the dressing compartment was equally convenient. Some of the drawing-room cars are as luxurious as those of royal or imperial carriages on European lines, with mirrors, lounges, chandeliers, piano and bookcases. A novelty in some of the cars on the Pacific Line is an outside balcony from which the scenery can be surveyed.

In America the ingenuity of the directors seems to be exerted for the comfort of the poorest classes. The carriages are large and well venti-

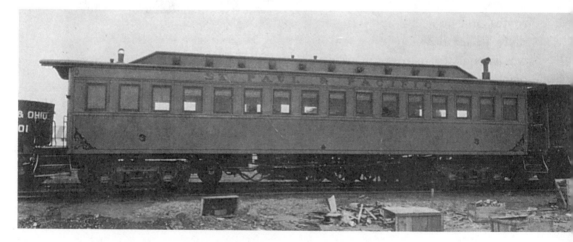

St. Paul & Pacific coach, about 1870 (by courtesy of the Baltimore & Ohio Railroad)

lated, with stoves for wintry weather and Venetian blinds and sun shades at every window in Summer. The seats are roomy and well cushioned. For parcels or small packages there are plenty of pegs and wire racks, and there is a barrel of filtered water, iced in Summer, at one end of the car. Notwithstanding all this, there is room for improvement. The jumping and jolting on many of the lines is terrible. The rails are laid upon big wooden sleepers which seem often of needless irregularity in level. Great is the dust and glare in hot weather and the draft in cold weather. Except in the larger towns and at the hotel stations the dépôts are generally very plain wooden structures, with few fixings and at night cheerless and ill lighted.

∽◕ 1 8 7 3 ◕∾

THE BAGGAGE-SMASHERS OF OMAHA

[From *Western Wanderings*, J. W. Boddam-Whetham (London, 1874), pp. 16, 17, 28, 29, 30, 44, 50, 57, 101]

We took the Erie Railroad from New York to Niagara as it seemed by the map to pass through a more picturesque country than the other routes, and on a dull damp morning ensconced ourselves in a Pullman silver palace drawing-room and hotel-car. Such a high sounding title was enough to take one's breath away. It reminded me of a palace scene in the Arabian nights. The reality, however, was simply a long railway carriage with chairs like music stools with arms; some nets of a size quite incapable of holding anything and a brilliant array of spittoons. Nor must I forget the filter of water, with one glass or tin cup chained to it, out of which everybody from the peanut boy and porters were supposed to drink. For the privilege of entering these luxurious structures an extra three dollars per day had to be paid.

At Port Jervis a most voluble old lady entered the car bringing with her an extraordinary assortment of luggage. She had two bandboxes, a dog, a flower pot, an umbrella, a jug of milk, a lunch basket, a parcel of figs and a boy of fifteen whose age she gave at the ticket-office as nine. I heard her tell her nearest neighbor of the fact and she chuckled over it as if she had performed a most virtuous action.

As our sleeping-car afforded no signs of sleeping accommodations I waited with curiosity for bedtime. It came at last and the chambermaid in the shape of a black man entered and asked me to move as he was going to make up the beds. He then made up the beds, all the arrangements of which were very good in themselves but there was no possible way of making use of them with the smallest degree of comfort. If there had only been a few hooks for hanging hats, coats and other garments upon and a place to put boots in it would have been something to be thankful for. For usually boots were to be found in the morning at different ends of the car or else on the wrong person's feet.

The space between the upper and lower berth does not allow of the occupant of the bed sitting up; the double windows are kept shut that he may not be smothered in dust and ashes and the night is passed in the most luxurious misery. The man who slept in the berth next to mine snored frightfully; in fact, night was made hideous by the unmusical sounds issuing from all parts of the car. The horrors of that first night in a Pullman car are indelibly impressed on my mind. The atmosphere ran a close heat with that of the Black Hole of Calcutta. On my asking the porter why he kept a fire burning all night he said he had to sit up and it would never do for him to catch cold.

If going to bed is misery, getting up in the morning is simply agony. If you are late you have to wait some hours before you can get a turn at the one washbasin. If you are early you have to stand outside on the platform in the dust and smoke until the beds are once more metamorphosed into seats, there being no room or other place to retire to until that operation is performed.

. . . . . .

We chose the Burlington and Quincy Railroad for the trip from Chicago to Omaha and again had the pleasure of looking forward to another night in a sleeping-car. On one section our car bumped about in a most extraordinary manner. On looking back at the long lines of rails over which we had just passed they seemed so unevenly laid, so rugged with ups and downs that it was a wonder how we kept on the rails at all. One of the passengers remarked to the conductor that the road seemed rather rough. "Well, yes," he answered, "trains do jump about some, but it's enough for us if they keep between the fences." However, we managed not only to keep between the fences but actually on the track and gradually approached the town of Council Bluffs. We very soon had enough of Council Bluffs and crossed the muddy river on a fine iron bridge to Omaha.

I was glad to get away from Omaha without having my luggage entirely knocked to pieces, as Omaha is celebrated for its baggage-smashers. There were several boxes lying about whose owners could only recognize them by their contents. Many a handsome box must have left Chicago as a Saratoga and arrived at San Francisco mere lumber.

We did not see any buffalos until we passed a station called Brady Island. There a fine herd was feeding along the banks of the river, well in the open and far removed from any chance of a surprise. It was a relief to see the long looked for animals at last, for only those who have felt it can understand what a dreadful thing it is to want to see a buffalo and not be able to do so.

The eating-stations all along the route call for great improvement; some of them are moderately good but as a rule the food is ill cooked and worse served. Morning, noon and night the same cry greets you at every meal: mutton-chop, beef-steak, ham and eggs! No change of any sort from the time you leave New York until you arrive at San Fancisco.

Everybody has heard and too many have partaken of the dry chops, the gutta-percha steaks, the bean-coffee and the current leaf tea to be found at railway eating-places. There are desperate skirmishes with the waiter who persists in bringing tea when you want coffee and who tells you, " It's all the same, sir "; the struggles for the bread or sugar and if you be late the hateful cry of " All aboard! " ringing in your ears and obliging you to rush off, leaving the proprietor counting his money and arranging the victuals for the next batch. It is wonderful how expert the people who keep these places become in collecting money. Needless to say, the ubiquitous pie is to be found in all its glory in these places. The number of victims to intemperance in pie-eating must be enormous. A light hand for pastry would be useless in making these pies; a hand that can manufacture a pie, every inch of which means a nightmare for a week, is the one most in request.

Ten minutes for refreshments (copyright by The Great Atlantic & Pacific Tea Company, Inc.)

I have often wondered how people who cannot afford the high fares of the Pullman cars get through the long journey from New York to San Francisco. The ordinary cars are without carpets, the seats are often without cushions and not a place for a sick man or child to lie down day or night and no room for change of position. Crowded indiscriminately with whites, blacks and Chinese, people of cultivated minds and habits have to herd with the vulgar and low-mannered and the journey altogether must be as near an approach to a seven day's purgatory as is possible.

THE SILVER PALACE SLEEPING CARS

[From *Teresina in America*, Therese Yelverton, Viscountess
Avonmore (London, 1875), II, 4-10]

I met with no silver whatever in the Silver Palace sleeping-cars. The
fittings, lamps, bolts, hinges, door handles, etc. are of the white metal
called pinchbeck or Britannia metal, and the palaces are fitted up in
the ordinary hotel style, the floors carpeted and oil-clothed and the seats
velvet-covered.

There are no special cars for ladies and if your opposite neighbor is
a gentleman in the day, in all probability you will have him on your
shelf at night and it will be well for you if he does not either snore
or have nightmare. Although you have blankets, sheets and pillows you
have to go to bed in your boots, at least ladies have to, and indeed they
cannot undress at all because they cannot shroud themselves behind
the curtains without placing themselves in a recumbent position. Besides, what could be done with their clothing? It could only be put on
the bed and already stowed away there are hand bags, books, umbrellas,
goloshes, wraps, tins of biscuits and possibly a large flask of Bourbon.

Everyone is obliged to retire to rest at a certain hour and rise ditto, for
all the beds must go up and come down together. Then follows waiting
one's turn at the silver lavatory, which consists of two basins, a palatial
roller-towel and a piece of soap. There is a silver tap whence you
procure clean water—and wash the basin too if a score of your neighbors
have used it before you. Particular people select the cleanest portion
of the towel or carry their own. In the same luxurious manner you are
accommodated with comb, brush, nailbrush and toothbrush. I saw a
lady take from her pocket a very handsome set of teeth, clean them
carefully with the brush provided by the company, and place the teeth
in her mouth. "I don't sleep in them," she remarked. "It uses them
out so bad and they are right expensive."

The lavatory is situated at the entrance of the car and cannot be made
private either from without or within, and anything like a good wash

is out of the question. You cannot even tuck up your hair or roll up your sleeves but some gentleman or conductor is sure to pounce upon you and remark, " Very refreshing to get a good wash." After this vain attempt at ablution you return to your seat, where you can order breakfast, for the bed has disappeared and a small slide is drawn out over which a white cloth is spread. The bill-of-fare is produced and you can breakfast and dine just as you would on a sea voyage. Fresh vegetables may run short but everything that can be pickled, preserved or carried in cans you can order. Bread and cake are baked twice a day in the train and are always hot. With your breakfast comes the morning paper, the *Great Pacific Line Gazette*, printed on board each day, narrating all the items of news of the preceding one, also a love story. The passengers are allowed to contribute and can advertise for lost articles.

I need not dilate upon the effect of thirty or forty human beings being boxed up together for seven days and nights, crammed close to each other all day, sleeping on shelves at night and in the same atmosphere. It is dangerous to seek relief by going from the overheated cars to the intense cold outside and if an attempt be made to let in a little fresh air by the window some one is sure to have the toothache.

The insufferable tedium of sitting in one position and even staring at the same persons for so long a time gives you a sort of nervous fidget. You can vary this monotony by a walk down the middle passage but the cars sway so much that if you have not sea-legs you are sure to tumble over some one or some one over you. Worse still, you may fall against the hot stove or the water tank with which every car is provided. These water tanks are the end and aim of most people's promenade and the tin cup is in constant requisition, for there is no stint of iced-water. Gentlemen amuse themselves by walking the full length of the train and jumping from platform to platform of the different cars. There is a smoking car, and cards, etc., form also an amusement, but I think that few people who have spent a week in these palaces on rails would ever wish to spend another.

LEAKS IN THE PULLMAN

[From *Dottings Round the Circle*, Benjamin Robbins Curtis
(Boston, 1877), pp. 5, 8, 9, 10, 11]

We leave Niagara Falls at 1 P.M., July 5, by the Michigan Central and
Great Western Railroad and after a somewhat tedious and uninteresting
day's journey we arrive at Detroit at 10 P.M. Today we made our first
trial of a hotel-car and although the dinner is hot and the food well
cooked and of good quality, the dust and cinders pretty effectually
spoil the repast, for, as the kitchen occupies a large share of these hotel-
cars, it is almost impossible to keep the windows closed.

We reach Kansas City at 8:30 P.M. July 9, and find the train for
Denver waiting nearby on the Kansas Pacific Railroad. We start at
ten o'clock and soon after are rushing over the desolate prairies. As
far as the eye can see on either side of the train there stretches one flat,
unbroken, barren waste of land with scarcely a living thing to break
the intense silence and dreadful monotony. Once in about two hours
the train halts at a station, consisting of one dwelling-house, a saloon
and a few lazy looking Indians, and after taking in a fresh supply of
water and fuel we leave all this behind us with no great regrets. Wearied
with the monotony, I go forward to the engine and persuade the engineer to let me ride with him. From here I can at least see all that the
country has to show.

We are due in Denver at 6 P.M. July 10, but at the last station where
we halt for dinner we receive the annoying news by telegraph that the
thunderstorm of yesterday has washed away two bridges between us
and Denver and a long delay is inevitable. Fortunately, we are halted
at a little place called Hugo, where food can be obtained. What a comfortless position! Standing still, away out on a desolate prairie in a
drenching rain—drenching, for the roof of our Pullman leaks badly and
all we can do is follow the porter's advice and wait till it swells. We
finally arrive at Denver at 8 P.M. on July 11, having been on the road
from Kansas City forty-eight hours.

Everyone coming to Denver hears of its excellent hotels long before his arrival. The Grand Central, the Interocean, the Sargent House and others are the best, indeed, between St. Louis and Salt Lake City. Not knowing, of course, exactly where they are located in the city, he will be somewhat surprised on his arrival at the station to see directly opposite across the square a row of small wooden hotels, each one bearing one of these well known names, its namesake being in reality located in a distant part of the town. Unless one is on the lookout for this deception it may happen that you take up your abode in one of these catchpennies before you discover your mistake. This state of things should be suppressed by the municipal authorities.

〜∘ 1 8 7 6 ᧞〜

A TOURIST'S GUIDEBOOK

[From *The Pacific Tourist*, Henry T. Williams (New York, 1876), pp. 8-13]

In no part of the world is travel made so comfortable and easy as on the Pacific Railroad. To travelers from the East it is a constant delight and to ladies and families it is accompanied with absolutely no fatigue or discomfort. One lives at home in the palace-car with as much true enjoyment as in the home drawing-room and with the constant change of scenes afforded from the car window it is far more enjoyable than the saloon of a fashionable steamer. For an entire week or more, as the train leisurely crosses the continent, the little section and berth allotted to you, so neat and clean, so nicely furnished and kept, becomes your home. Here you sit and read, play your games, indulge in social conversation and glee, and if fortunate enough to possess friends to join you the overland tour becomes an intense delight.

The sleeping-cars from New York to Chicago, proceeding at their rushing rate of forty or more miles an hour, give to travelers no idea of the true comfort of Pullman-car life. From Chicago westward to Omaha the cars are finer and traveling more luxurious, likewise the rate of speed is slower and the motion of the train more easy than on roads farther east. At Omaha, as you view the long Pacific train, often over 600 feet in length, just ready to leave the dépôt for its overland trip, you can but admit it is exceedingly beautiful and impressive.

The slow rate of speed, which averages but sixteen to twenty miles an hour day and night, produces a peculiarly smooth, gentle and easy motion, most soothing and agreeable. The straight track, which for hundreds of miles is without a curve, avoids all swinging motion of the cars and sidelong bumps are unknown. The cars are connected with the Miller buffer and platform, and make a solid train without the discomforts of jerks and jolts. And the steady, easy jog of the train as it leisurely moves westward gives a feeling of genuine comfort such as no one ever feels or enjoys in any other part of the world.

To enjoy palace-car life properly one always needs a good companion, so you can take a section together. From Chicago to Omaha the company in sleeping-cars is usually quiet and refined, but beyond Omaha there is often an indescribable mixture of races in the same car and if you are alone the chance is that your *compagnon du voyage* may not be agreeable. It is impossible to order a section for one person alone and the dictum of the sleeping-car arrangements at Omaha requires all who come to take what berths are assigned.

Fee your porter on the sleeping-car twenty-five cents a day. The porters of both Pacific railroads are esteemed especially excellent, obliging and careful.

Travelers need make no preparations for eating on the cars, as meals at all dining-halls are excellent and food of great variety is nicely served, such as buffalo meat, antelope steak, tongue of all kinds and the best of beefsteaks. Lunch-counters are attached to all eating-stations, so that you may easily procure hot coffee, tea, biscuits, sandwiches and fruit if you do not wish a full meal. The uniform price of all meals at overland stations is one dollar in greenbacks, but on the Central Pacific you can pay 75 cents in silver if you prefer.

For your clothing on the overland trip you will need at Omaha the first day, if it is Summer, a light Spring suit, and a Winter suit the next day at Sherman. Again at Salt Lake City and the Humbolt Desert the thinnest of Summer suits and at the summit of the Sierras all your underclothing. We can only advise you as you pass through so many extremes of temperature to always wear your underclothing, day and night, throughout the trip and add an overcoat if the air grows chilly.

All baggage of reasonable weight can be checked from any Eastern city direct to Council Bluffs. At Council Bluffs it is re-checked and weighed and a charge of 15 cents a pound is made on all in excess of 100 pounds.

The tariff to travelers with all companies is as follows, in greenbacks:

One berth, New York to Chicago	$5.00 by any route.
One berth, Chicago to Omaha	3.00 by any route.
One berth, Omaha to Ogden	8.00 by the Union Pacific.
One berth, Ogden to San Francisco	6.00 by the Central Pacific.

⤳ 1 8 7 8 ⤳

A MUSICAL EVENING IN THE PALMYRA

[From *Through America*, W. G. Marshall (London, 1882), pp. 59-71, 129-136, 238-247]

After breakfast on June 1, we took the 9:30 train for Niagara, distance 328 miles from Albany. At Utica, in the middle of the day, we all turned out to dine except one old gentleman in our car, who preferred remaining behind and contenting himself with dining off his cigar. He had a peaceful chew all to himself while we did full justice to the good things at the station buffet.

Our train consists of two baggage-cars placed next to the engine and behind them the mail-car containing all the letters. It has a little letter-box at the side called a dispatch-box, into which you can slip a newspaper or a letter at any time during the journey and have it duly delivered. Every mail-train carries a dispatch-box and people are frequently running up and posting their letters in this way. Behind the mail-car came four passenger-cars and it is possible to walk through the train from one end to the other, beginning with the first baggage-car behind the engine and so on through to the doorway in the end of the last car, where you can stand and admire the receding view. I have met with the English form of railway car only once in America and that was on the Old Colony Railroad, which runs between Fall River, Taunton and Boston.

The seats in the ordinary cars all face one way, namely the engine, but if the seat in front of you is unoccupied you can if you like appropriate it with your legs by turning round the back of the seat on its hinges and lying at full length. On the Pennsylvania Railroad, however, notices are put up in the car informing you that this is positively prohibited. Pullman cars are generally used on the American railways and where they are not called by the name of Pullman they are constructed and fitted up in a similar manner. The arrangements in the sleeping-cars are so excellent that they leave nothing to be desired, and the gildings and paintings are of the highest order in point of elegance and taste.

A new conductor comes on board the train at each division of the line and proceeds at once to walk through the cars and examine all the tickets. After he has inspected your ticket, which you have purchased at the railroad's ticket-office or at your hotel, he will pocket it and give you in exchange a check which will have a notice like " Please keep this check in sight " printed on one side and on the other side all the stations of the division and the distances between them. Once, when traveling on the Shore Line from New York to Boston, the conductor of one of the divisions of that line presented me with a check on one side of which was printed as follows:

If you want a quiet nap,
Place this on your hat or cap.
And always by day or night,
Please keep this check in sight.

In the parlor-car we occupied today a Negro presided over a pantry which was at one end of it and dealt out for consumption fruit, strawberries and cream, tea, coffee, milk, lemonade, gin, sherry cobblers, sour mash cocktails, gin cocktails, mint juleps and an immense variety of iced drinks. He seemed to have a ready and endless supply of everything in this line of trade.

At eleven o'clock at night we reach the town of Niagara. Running the gauntlet of fourteen hotel runners, we manage after some difficulty in reaching the bus of the Clifton House and were quickly driven off to it.

. . . . . .

Thirty miles beyond Julesburg on the Union Pacific Railroad we came to Sidney, an eating-station and therefore a place of importance. We stopped half an hour to hurry out and get breakfast. Tearing into the station house past a man standing at the doorway who was vigorously proclaiming on a loud sounding gong that the feast was ready prepared and spread within, we found ourselves in a room furnished with many neatly arrayed tables. We had plenty of the gentler sex to wait on us. There was plenty of time to eat and plenty of room to spare. There were given us eight little dishes apiece containing hot beefsteak, two slices of cold roast antelope, a bit of cold chicken, ham and poached eggs, a couple of boiled potatoes, two sticks of sweet corn, stewed tomatoes and four thin buckwheat hot cakes laid one on top of the other, to be eaten with golden syrup the last thing of all.

We were all served alike; everyone was given the same as his neighbor. Knives and forks were lamentably scarce, as usual. One knife and fork to each to last through the whole meal is the order of the day out here. Cold tea in tumblers with a quantity of sugar added seemed to constitute the popular beverage, if it was not cold milk. There was hot tea and coffee for those who preferred. All ate as if for their very lives and the result was that we were all through together a quarter of an hour before it was time to start. For this and for every meal, except two, along the route of the Pacific Railroad from Omaha to San Francisco the charge is one dollar.

A few miles beyond Hazard we pull up on a side track at a shanty named Otto to allow the Eastern overland train to pass us. The two trains pull up close by the side of each other and greetings are exchanged between the respective conductors and baggage-masters. Our newspaper man hands over to the newspaper man of the eastbound train a bundle of the latest issues of the Chicago and Omaha papers and in return we are presented with the latest issues of the San Francisco and Salt Lake journals. One is as anxious to get hold of a paper out here to ascertain the latest news as one is after a week at sea. Anything to break the monotony of the long ride over the Plains!

On the platform at Laramie is a collection of fossils and minerals, heads of animals shot in the vicinity, and other interesting curiosities. Collections such as these are to be found at all the eating-stations on this part of the Overland Route and the prices asked for the several specimens could not be called excessive. At Laramie we had supper and then proceeded fifty miles to Rock Creek, where we had another supper. Resuming our journey once more, night overtakes us. We have a little eight-stop organ in our sleeping-car the *Palmyra* and this evening we bring out its tone and our companions in the car contribute a few songs. The instrument has two manuals but will only sound in one and the upper part is devoted to pillow cases and blankets. So for two hours we amuse ourselves with singing and playing, our conductor, who was a bit of a musician in his way, coming and treating us to a few songs. I believe if we had only had room enough we should have got up a dance, but this was entirely out of the question. In this way we spent a very pleasant evening.

We pulled up at Wahsatch station to allow the Eastern overland train to pass us. As it was a little behind time, our conductor amused himself

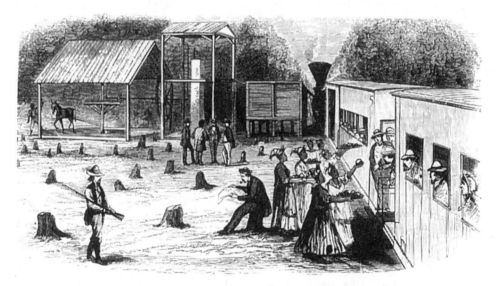

Tourists en route to Florida in 1874. A mule-operated pump supplying water for the locomotive (from *Frank Leslie's Illustrated Weekly*, December 5, 1874)

by taking shots at one of the telegraph posts with his revolver and about a half dozen of us followed suit and fired at the same.

On June 11, 1878 we left Salt Lake City for San Francisco, a distance of 920 miles. After a run of thirty-seven miles over ground we had already traversed, a distance we managed to accomplish in two hours, stopping at four small stations on the way, we reached Ogden. On reaching the station we were received by such a clanging and booming of gongs, together with such an uproarious babble of voices from a number of excited individuals directly we stepped out of the train, that it looked as if we had to come to a place where everyone had taken leave of his senses. What did it all mean? In a word, it meant dinner. There are four or five insignificant looking little inns hard by the Ogden station and the runners of these hotels, each armed with a big gong, came forth upon the arrival of our train and made the most of the windfall.

As we had a couple of hours to wait we began to turn a favorable ear to their vehement declarations, but so passionately did they address us and so violently did they abuse one another that I thought more than once that there was going to be a free fight. One of them promised us a clean meal for seventy-five cents, one promised us one for fifteen cents less and offered to get in addition some young ladies to wait on us. A third promised us a fifty-cent dinner, young ladies to wait and a good bottle of wine besides. Needless to say, we closed with this last mentioned offer.

Dinner over, which was served half cold and what was served was half cooked, we returned to the station to see about securing a section in a sleeping-car. But as might have been expected, it was too late for us now to secure any berths. So the prospect was before us of having to make the best of the situation for two nights in an ordinary car, where not only would there be no proper accommodation for those who wished to sleep, but no provision of lavatories such as are in the parlor and sleeping-cars.

At 8:30 A.M. we reach Elko. Elko is an eating-station and we turn out for breakfast. A gong, as usual, proclaims loudly that the feast is quite ready, and we rush out of the train ahead of everybody, for, before eating, we have our toilets to attend to after such a night as we have been obliged to put up with. The white, salinous dust brushed up by the train came sweeping in at the doors of the car intermittently opened during the night and completely covered us, curled up though we were on the two seats of our section, with handkerchiefs tied around our necks and a rug thrown over us, making shift the best we could under the unpleasant circumstances. But everything had to be done in a hurry for we had only twenty minutes allowed us before our journey would have to be resumed. So when we were through with our ablutions we hurriedly seek the meal room which the uproarious clatter of knives and forks renders not very difficult to find. Politely conducted to our seats by a Chinaman, we indulge in a repast that might be called sumptuous, considering our location, and pay a dollar for it.

❧ 1 8 7 9 ❧

SIGNS AND BILLBOARDS

[From *Two Sides of the Atlantic*, James Burnley (London, 1880), pp. 52, 53, 54]

The dépôts in the large cities are large and sometimes handsome buildings but away from the great centers they are little better than barns, destitute of proper waiting-rooms and conveniences and having no platform worth the name. There is a naked, slovenly uncared for look about these dépôts and the attendance of porters is so scanty as scarcely to be worth mentioning.

Just before the train draws up at a station the brakeman pops his head into the car and makes a noise which, if you have knowledge beforehand, you may construe into the name of the station you are approaching, but which, if you are a stranger, you will most likely fail to comprehend. In this condition of ignorance you naturally crane your neck out of the window and look about for the name, expecting it to be emblazoned glaringly on some board or wall; but no, you look up and you look down and most probably there is no name at all. To the passenger who knows every station on the line this omission does not matter much, but to the stranger it is of the utmost consequence.

On leaving the dépôt the train goes past street corners, past houses and shops, up streets and down streets like any other ordinary object of traffic. The lines are not fenced off, as a rule, nor are there any strict regulations observed as to crossings. As an American put it to me, " The railroads in this country are constructed under the impression that the people who move about amongst them are in possession of their senses. Why shouldn't a man have to exercise his faculties in saving himself from being run down by a locomotive as well as from being run over by a wagon or a coach? The engine makes noise enough, surely."

But in respect to animals some consideration is extended, inasmuch as every animal that is slaughtered by the train has to be paid for by the company. It thus happens that the free passage of trains out in the great grazing districts where cattle herd together by the thousands and roam across the open track at will becomes a difficult matter. Out on the prairies the slackenings, whistlings and stoppages to avoid destroying cattle are of very frequent occurrence and you see the animals trooping off to the right and left of the line every few minutes.

The American business man believes in advertising on or near railways and he does it to an extent that is somewhat disagreeable. He probably would have the stations decorated with a neatly framed display-board indicating his world wide celebrity as a tailor or the magical properties of his stove polish but for the simple reason that most of the stations are lost to all possibility of decoration. But at all risks he is determined to catch the eye of the railway traveler and he does it. Wherever there is a bit of fence, a conspicuous gable end or a surface of wood, stone or brick that can be seen from the railroad and converted into a sign, there he will advertise himself and where there is no coign of advantage he will create one. He will build a sign fifteen or twenty yards long in the middle of the next field to the railway if he can do nothing else. Rising Sun Stove Polish haunts you by every railway side on the continent and as you ride you read a thousand other equally important announcements. The eyesight is annoyed at these things; the mind is troubled with them.

CONGRESSIONAL COURTESY

[From *The Other Side*, C. B. Berry (New York, 1880), pp. 38, 41, 45, 49, 53]

Bidding a regretful adieu to the Fifth Avenue Hotel, we left Desbrosses Street Station, Jersey City, at six o'clock one evening for Philadelphia. We had heard a great deal about the marvelous luxury and convenience of American trains and had been given to understand that a journey in the States was an experience of almost ecstatic bliss. " For unparalleled upholstery, the profusion of comfort and civility of employés our cars are without a compeer; no other cars are a patch upon them." Such had been the words of an enthusiastic citizen and we passively resigned ourselves to three hours of unheard of splendor.

We emerged from the ticket-office upon a shadowy expanse of dimly lighted terminus and made for the train. The rails were upon the same level as the platform; and the general aspect of affairs was that of a recent reclamation from the wilderness. Porters were conspicuous by their absence. We encountered a conductor who upon enquiry informed us that there was no smoking-car attached to the train but that we could smoke in the baggage-car.

The baggage-car proving merely a gloomy and cavernous receptacle for trunks, we therefore entered an ordinary car. The atmosphere resembled that of a limekiln, dry and baking, the effect of a large stove at each end, aggravated by all the windows being closely shut. The car had no division from end to end, a length of some fifty feet, while to light this large apartment the Pennsylvania Railway had generously provided two candles swung in glass globes as in the stateroom of a steamer. The dim religious light thus provided sufficed just to exhibit the extent of the darkness and was well suited to such as might desire to sleep, but 6 P.M. was rather early for a car full of people to seek repose. Then, as if in playful irony, a newsman appeared offering papers and magazines for sale. Sleep itself would have been perilous, since from the lowness of the seat backs the sleeper's head would have descended to the rear in an uncertain and suicidal manner.

Ten minutes later we are startled by the clamor of a most doleful bell and the train moves off. The bell continues its solemnizing tones and looking out of the window we find ourselves running through the middle of the street. There is no barrier between the line and the space left for street traffic and the people clear off the track with no other warning. There is a whistle on the engine but its use is prohibited in the dépôts or the streets.

We dashed through to Philadelphia at an express pace of twenty-five to thirty miles an hour, saddened at intervals by the tolling of the bell. Some time before arriving we were accosted by a gentleman who saw that we were strangers and very politely offered his services. This gentleman, whom we afterward found to be a member of Congress, gave us much pleasant information about the country through which we were passing and before parting invited us to his home in a Western city should we incline thither.

A very free and easy style prevails on the American train. People stand outside on the platform, walk from one car to another while the train is in motion, take an occasional turn into the baggage-car and consult their individual inclinations in every way. On a hot day in Summer they throw open all the windows to give free ingress to fresh air and dust, and the occupants of the smoking-car (there generally is one) sit with their feet tilted outside the window to woo the grateful breeze about their trouser legs.

The conductor and brakeman are important functionaries, the brakeman being the lesser luminary of the two. He sits at the end of his car among the passengers, running out to the platform to work the wheel as occasion demands. The conductor is a magnate of much presence. He is resplendent in uniform and buttons, has a peculiarly ugly cap, and weighs between 200 and 300 pounds. I hardly saw a conductor in the States whose girth could have been less than fifty inches. He would wither with a glance the unhappy man who ventured to offer him a tip.

Woodruff sleeping car, *Ida*, 1880

∽ 1 8 8 0 ↶

THE HOTEL CAR'S CULINARY DEPARTMENT

[From *Through Cities and Prairie Lands*, Lady Duffus Hardy
(New York, 1881), pp. 73, 74, 75, 80, 81, 82, 95]

Of the many routes to San Francisco we chose the Pennsylvania line
of railway, which takes us as far as Chicago, having been informed
by some old tourists that we should find it by far the most picturesque
and agreeable, besides being the smoothest to run over, the rails being
steel and laid with special care and the new cars being built with all
consideration for the convenience and comfort of the passengers. We
had rather a dread of the American railways, having heard so much of
their reckless speed and wilful disregard of all rules and regulations,
but we gained confidence as we discovered the surprising fact that life
is equally dear to its owners here as at home.

We settled ourselves comfortably in the seats of our luxurious Pullman car and prepared to enjoy the scenery. As the night closes in, the
excitement and novelty of our day's travel calms down and we turn
our attention to the internal arrangements of our temporary home and
are interested in watching our comfortable, velvet cushioned section

turned into a cozy sleeping place. Soft mattresses, snowy sheets and warm, gaily striped blankets are extracted from behind the ornamental panels overhead, the curtains are let down, and we may go to rest as soon as we please. But we do not please until we have consulted our conductor, whose sole occupation during the day has been walking to and fro the cars punching our tickets until they resemble a piece of perforated cardboard. If this process is to be carried on during the night we think we shall have small chance of rest but the matter is satisfactorily settled and we may sleep in peace.

Our trial came in the morning, when we marched to the dressing-room to perform our toilette and found a whole army of dishevelled females armed with toothbrushes, sponges, etc., besieging the four-foot space called the ladies dressing-room, each waiting for the first sign of surrender to march in and take possession. This was the miserable epoch in our daily lives through all the overland journey; in everything else our car life was delightfully luxurious and pleasant.

No hotel or dining-cars accompany the morning train from New York, but eating-stations are erected at certain portions of the road where you may get rid of the most wolfish appetite at an admirably spread table and plenty of time allowed for the knife and fork engagement. We reached Chicago that evening and were most kindly received at the Palmer House.

The next morning we started via the Chicago and Northwestern Railway for Omaha. This is a most desirable route over even, well laid rails and the cars are easy and luxurious, and we were whirled along over the illimitable prairie with a pleasant, gliding, almost noiseless motion. This, we were told, is owing to some invention of India rubber or paper wheels which the company has applied to their cars which greatly adds to the comfort of their travelers. It was here for the first time we enjoyed the luxury of the hotel-car. We were getting hungry and curious to know what good things the gods would provide for us.

Presently a good humored Negro clothed all in white brought us a bill-of-fare from which to select our meal. There were so many good things that we held a consultation as to what would form the most desirable meal. We decided on mulligatawney soup, broiled oysters, lamb cutlets and peas. A narrow passage, every inch of which is utilized, separates the kitchen from the rest of the car. How is it that in so many private houses the odor of roast and broil travels from the kitchen and insinuates itself into the remotest corner of the house? Here the occupants of the car but a few feet off have no suggestion of dinner till it is placed before them.

We were curious as to the working of the culinary department and animated by a noble desire to obtain knowledge we penetrated the sacred precincts of the cook. The kitchen was a perfect gem of a place about eight feet square. A range ran along one side, its dark shining face breaking out into an eruption of knobs, handles and hinges of polished brass or steel. Curious little doors were studded all over it. Pots, steamers and pans were simmering on the top. Every requisite for carrying on the gastronomical operations was there in that tiny space in the neatest and most compact form. Scrupulous cleanliness reigned supreme over all. There was the pantry with its polished silver, glass and china in shining array. The refrigerator, with a plentiful supply of ice, and the larder were side by side. The wine and beer cellar was artfully arranged beneath the car. Thus every inch of space was realized to its utmost extent.

Toward six o'clock every table was spread with dainty linen and the dinner was exquisitely served according to the previous order of each traveler. The simplest dish as well as the most elaborate was cooked to perfection and everybody fell to with a will! Early hours were kept here as in our other traveling home and the same routine was pursued in the morning. Breakfast was served about eight o'clock.

At Council Bluffs we were crammed into a long, comfortless wagon-like car with a host of nondescript folk. It was stuffy and by no means savory, for the windows were all closed to keep out the wind and the rain, which was now pouring in torrents. Slowly we begin to move, and are carried across the mile long bridge which spans the Missouri river and connects Omaha and Council Bluffs. At last we creak and rumble into the station at Omaha and as we glance around us we feel that we are on the threshold of a new world. The platform is crowded with a motley assemblage of people from which the genteel element seems to be wholly eliminated. The immigrant train has just arrived and disgorged its living freight. Having been penned up so long in such close quarters, they were glad to get out and stretch their legs and rinse the dirt from their grimy faces.

The Grand Pacific Hotel having been destroyed by fire, we get into an omnibus which conveys us to the Cosmopolitan, which is a striking contrast to the magnificent hotels which have hitherto lined our route. As we only intended to remain in Omaha for a day we walked out to take a view of the town. It is a most dreary, desolate looking city, with wide straggling dusty streets and next to nobody in them. The shops are numerous enough, such as they are, but nobody is doing anything; there seems to be nothing to do. I was not sorry when our twenty-four hours in Omaha were over.

We start once more on our pleasant Pullman-car. We arrange our tiny packages and make ourselves as much as possible at home in our cozy section. The car is crowded, as the different lines of railway end here and all who are westward bound must come on this one daily train from Omaha. Having taken note of our fellow passengers, we lean back in our seats and look out upon the vast prairie which rolls before and around us like a gray-green motionless sea. So time passes till we reach Cheyenne. There we all turn out in anticipation of having a thoroughly good meal and are not disappointed. We enjoy a capital dinner. The hot soup is excellent; then we have boiled trout and a roast of black-tailed deer, the most delicious flavored, tender meat conceivable, fresh vegetables and fruit are plentifully supplied, and as a crowning bliss we enjoy the luxury of black coffee.

Everybody is content and everybody has a good word for Cheyenne. Why is it that things are not equally well managed throughout this well traveled route? As a rule, the eating-stations are wretchedly supplied.

We have thrown away many a noble appetite on tough, tasteless steak and watery soup that had scarcely strength to run down our throats. A well filled lunch-basket is a necessity, a comfort as well as an economy, for the charges at these places are a dollar for anything unless you crowd to the immigrants' refreshment bar, where cooking is by no means studied as a high art.

It is quite dark when we steam into the station at Ogden. The gong is sounding an invitation to dinner of which we are glad enough to avail ourselves. Porters are dashing about with lighted lanterns, luggage is wheeled across the platform to the other train for there is a general change at this point and all passengers are shifted from the Union Pacific which ends here, to the Central Pacific, which takes up the journey westward. An hour is allowed for dinner and soon the now familiar cry, " All aboard! " greets our ears and after a few hurried good-byes the westward bound speed on their way. We have decided to remain for the night and we have the whole place to ourselves. Our resting place is sandwiched between the two lines of the Union and Central Pacific. It is a long, narrow, wooden building only two stories high, the lower floor being devoted to railroad business and a large dining-room and the upper floor consisting of ten or twelve cozy white-curtained sleeping-rooms. We would advise everyone to rest there for a night on their way westward; it forms a delightful break in their journey.

꒰ꙮ 1 8 8 2 ꙮ꒱

BREAKFAST IN THE DINER

[From *A Scamper Through America*, T. S. Hudson (New York, 1882), pp. 78, 79, 80, 82, 83]

We left Washington for the West in the forenoon, taking parlor-car tickets for Cumberland and sleeper tickets thence to Cincinnati for the night traveling. A great source of inconvenience in traveling is what appears to be the foolish arrangement of clocks. An attempt is made by every large place to use solar time, hence trains are made to run as nearly as possible to the time of the sun. In the forty hours' ride now commenced we had three times—Washington, Vincennes and St. Louis. It became absolutely indispensable to carry with our watches a reconciliation card with little dials showing the hour at a dozen different places when noon at New York.

The only way to be certain of catching a train is always to be at the station very early, particularly if you have luggage. There is a great deal of delay about checking the latter and there is needless time wasted at both ends but the system is very safe. No encouragement is given to taking parcels in the cars with you and care must be taken to have just so much impedimenta with you as you can conveniently carry as there are no porters to transport you from platform to platform or from train to cab. I use the word platform, but the boards from which you enter the cars are laid level with the ground. Traveling trunks must be strongly made as the fellows who handle them are called smashers and well they earn their appellation.

The time-tables provided by each line contain, within a highly colored wrapper, the times, distances, fares and altitudes on one side and on the other a map showing the particular railroad and its connections. The latter is very useful; a trifling fault being that the company's own line, marked by a thick black line across the map, is invariably shown to be as nearly as possible as the crow flies, whereas competing lines appear to be more devious than they actually are.

After a night spent in our traveling couches we were up with the sun and after toilet and ablutions, for which the car provided tolerable facilities, we arrived at Cincinnati for a two hours' stroll round the city, during which we saw and smelt quite sufficient of the capital of Ohio.

At eight o'clock, once more aboard bound westward, we partook of a good breakfast, cooked and served on the train. The following menu was distributed through the cars:

As you journey through Life Live by the Way.

BREAKFAST

Now Ready
Served in first class Style
Price 75 cents.

A DINING CAR
Is attached to this train

Eat and be satisfied.

PASSENGERS

Will appreciate this new feature of
Life on the Road

Breakfast Bill of Fare

English Breakfast Tea   French Coffee   Chocolate   Ice Milk

Bread

French Loaf   Boston Brown Bread   Corn Bread   Hot Rolls, Dry, dipped, cream toast

Broiled

Tenderloin steak, plain or with Mushrooms   Spring Chicken   Mutton Chops
Veal Cutlets   Sirlon Steak   Sugar-Cured Ham
Game in their Season
Oysters in their Season

Fried

Calf's Liver with Bacon   Country Sausage   Trout

Eggs

Fried   Scrambled   Boiled   Omelets   Plain

Relishes

Radishes   Chow Chow   French Mustard   Current Jelly   Walnut Catsup   Mixed Pickles

Vegetables

Stewed, Fried and Boiled Potatoes

Fruits

Apples   Oranges

The stoppages at the two hundred and fifty stations were lengthy and the whole journey very leisurely, occupying six days and nights from ocean to ocean, whereas it could be done in four to four and a half. Doubtless the through traffic and that between the great centers is not sufficient to support a fast train each way daily, and so what is termed the express serves a local traffic which is no doubt remunerative and also renders the traveling for through passengers more interesting and possibly less fatiguing than a mere flash across the continent.

∽ 1 8 8 3 ⌒

BAGGAGE-SMASHING AS AN ART

[From *East to West*, Henry W. Lucy (London, 1885), pp. 148, 149, 156, 158]

An inconvenience inseparable from the distance run on American railways is the variation in time. Going West, one's watch is always slowing; going East, it gains—a difficulty that might be grappled with if it stood alone. But there is superadded the uncertainty as to what time prevails in the connecting link of railway with which you are specially concerned. There was much disgust expressed on a Denver train at the discovery made, on reference to the time-table, that the Denver & Rio Grande Railway delivered its passengers at Ogden a quarter of an hour after the Central Pacific train had gone on to San Francisco. On arriving at Ogden it was found, on the contrary, that there was a good hour to spare for breakfast, the simple explanation being that, at Ogden, San Francisco time is taken up, whereas we had been running on Denver time. At Ogden trains running West are ruled by San Francisco time, which is 3 hr. 2 m. slower than Washington time, 3 hr. 26 m. than Boston, 3 hr. 14 m. than New York, 2 hr. 20 m. than Chicago, 2 hr. 9 m. than St. Louis, 1 hr. 46 m. than Omaha, and 42 m. slower than Ogden time. The waiting-room at Ogden is crowded with clocks giving the various times upon which divers trains will run. A scheme has been proposed and is now practically approved by the railway managers of dividing the breadth of the States into four parallels and changing the time by an hour as each of these is crossed.

The delay in American trains is truly Continental. Arriving at Salt Lake City from Denver, we were four hours late and starting next day from Ogden by the Central Pacific we had to wait three hours and a half for the arrival of the Union Pacific from the East. From Ogden to San Francisco is over eight hundred miles, a run in which there are possibilities of making up the loss of time, more especially when the average speed is twenty miles an hour. On this journey it was done and we reached San Francisco on time. But this is not always the case, as appears from the Denver journey quoted, the through passengers from the West missing their train and being compelled to stop at Ogden all night.

The railway porters treat each individual piece of baggage as if they owed it a personal grudge. Easy as it may seem to take the lightest and frailest boxes as the basis of a pile and then bring down upon them the iron-bound edges of a Saratoga trunk, it requires a great deal of skill and practice to so deal with whole carloads of luggage. Yet I have never seen at any station along four thousand miles of railway a single instance of failure. Tipping not being the practice, the railway porter has nothing to look for or hope for and accordingly takes it out on the baggage. This same absence of tips is doubtless responsible for the brusqueness, frequently reaching the stage of downright rudeness, which marks the manner of all with whom travelers have to deal at railway stations.

The American dépôt is simply a wilderness of rails level with the waiting-rooms. The train is halted in various positions on the broad, level highway, oftenest either in the middle or at the far side. No attempt is made to see that the passengers who have paid for their tickets start with the train. " All aboard! " the conductor confidentially observes to himself, and thereupon, without warning whistle or sound-ing bell, the train glides out of the station with whatever proportion of passengers may chance to be seated at the moment or in the frantic rush which follows may succeed in jumping on. If a train an hour or two late pulls up at a station and presently, moving off without a warning note, leaves a passenger behind, he is said to have " got himself left," which exactly represents the situation.

It is a matter of great regret to travelers that Mr. Baedeker forbears to include the United States in his familiar series of handbooks. There are handbooks in the United States, but they are curiously useless. I had one called " The Tourist's Guide to the United States and Canada " and for some days covering thousands of miles of travel it possessed a strange fascination for me, being the premier book in the English tongue as containing the least amount of information in proportion to its bulk.

༄ 1 8 8 3 ༄

A RUFUS HATCH TOUR TO THE YELLOWSTONE

[From *A Trip to America*, William Hardman (London, 1884), pp. 101-140]

Our departure from Chicago was the real commencement of our journey into the great Northwest. It was then that we found ourselves for the first time in the railway train which was to be more or less our home for the next three weeks, barring the time spent in the Yellowstone district.

Immediately behind the engine was a capacious car for our luggage and for the stores, fruit, vegetables, cases of champagne, claret, apollinaris and lager beer and other things necessary for the luxurious existence which we enjoyed. Next came the dining-car, with kitchen, pantry, store-room and ten tables, five on each side to accommodate four persons each. After that followed four Pullman sleeping-cars and after them the private car of Mr. John C. Wyman, the orator of our party, a gentleman of remarkable eloquence and geniality, always amusing us with some fresh joke or story. Finally, at the tail of the train was what is called an observation-car, with a platform at the end where such passengers as did not mind dust might sit and enjoy the scenery as we passed along. From this platform to the engine there was a complete thoroughfare through the middle of the cars, the only troublesome part being the crossing from car to car.

Punctually at 7:30 A.M. the serving of breakfast began, at one o'clock we had luncheon, and the dinner hour was six. The colored attendants who acted as chambermaids began to make up the beds soon after nine o'clock and by eleven everybody was fast asleep. It was a very strange sight to see these darkies at their bedmaking. Their rapidity and dexterity were marvelous. Their civility and attention, too, were beyond praise.

At half past nine in the morning we moved out of Chicago and arrived at St. Paul at eight o'clock the following morning, having completed the journey of 529 miles from Chicago in twenty-two and a half hours, including stoppages. Our average pace was under thirty miles an hour, not an excessive rate of speed, but we were delayed by what is technically known as a hot-box.

Our cars each had a name, such as Fargo, Minneapolis, Wamduska, Pyramid Park or Billings. I happened to inhabit a section in the coach known as Billings, a new and very comfortable vehicle, but as often happens with new cars one of its wheels worked stiffly. The result of this was the overheating of the box and several times during the night the train had to be stopped in order to extinguish the flames.

It was 8:30 that night before we started from St. Paul. We were now for the first time on the Northern Pacific Railroad, along which we were to travel for the rest of our journey. When I left Chicago I was told that I must be prepared to rough it, but at St. Paul and

Minneapolis, hundreds of miles away, comfort and luxury of every kind still surrounded me. Many miles had yet to be traversed before the roughing it commenced.

We reached the boundary of the State of Minnesota at daybreak and at six o'clock our train came to a standstill at Fargo. It was Sunday morning and in accordance with Mr. Rufus Hatch's inexorable rule we were never allowed to travel on Sunday. Our train was switched on to a siding and we prepared to spend the day. We were received with great cordiality by the leading citizens, who did everything in their power to make us welcome. Mr. Cooley preached us an excellent sermon on the Good Samaritan and made an earnest appeal for funds for the enlargement of the church.

I believe it was at Gladstone that we came upon a very shabby looking party of Indians standing on the platform hoping for a lift on their road west. They were of the Gros Ventre tribe and were on their way to hold a powwow with their friends the Crows. Mr. Rufus Hatch, kind-hearted as usual, offered them a seat on the observation platform of the last car as far as Little Missouri about fifty-three miles further on. We all crowded to look at them and some of the ladies of our party bought bracelets, bags and pincushions. All on board the train were heartily glad when we, not without difficulty, induced these hideous, dirty, sly-looking imbeciles to land at Little Missouri which we reached just before sunset.

There were not wanting skeptics in our party whose spirits drooped lower and lower as day after day went by and our train still sped on and only boundless and monotonous prairies were in view. We breakfasted, lunched, played whist, dined, smoked, sang, recited, told tales, guessed riddles and puzzles, played cards again, went to bed, got up the next morning to find much the same scenery and no apparent progress toward our journey's end. How long would this last? And should we be really rewarded by the wonders in " the Park "? Five days and nights have been spent in our train since leaving St. Paul.

Next morning at 5:30 our train plunged into the Gate of the Mountains, and a ride of three hours or more brought us to the end of the track. The rails are laid for a mile or two further but for some reason or other we were turned out here.

TICKET SCALPERS

[From *A Year in the Great Republic*, E. Catherine Bates (London, 1887), pp. 19, 23, 38, 40]

Our start for Boston from Niagara gave us two new experiences, one of which was later to become almost universal. I refer to the extreme uncertainty and unpunctuality of the trains. This refers of course more especially to the Western States, but even in the East we soon ceased to chafe over a lost hour or two in any dépôt.

On this occasion the delay lasted for only some two hours and the chief practical inconvenience lay in the fact that the passengers had eaten up most of the provisions *en route* from Chicago, so we were turned out next morning at 6 A.M. to get food as best we might at some roadside station. In such a large country, where trains are constantly late, the commissariat department is apt to break down under the strain. Anyone who has been condemned to eat three meals a day at railroad stations may be safely fed on dried-up sandwiches or fossil buns for the remainder of his life and still be thankful.

Our other experience in regard to this journey was an explanation of the railway ticket-scalping business. Yesterday a man offered to get us tickets from Niagara to Boston for $9.25, the night fare being $11. There is enormous competition amongst the railway companies and it frequently happens that one or other gets into serious difficulties. The company is forced to raise money, so they sell a large amount of tickets to a speculator at a very much reduced rate. The man who buys them up gets rid of all he can at the recognized price, but as the time elapses over which the tickets are negotiable he is forced to offer them at lower rates and hence the great reduction which is often made upon them. On several occasions in the West, having had to pay as much for a ticket covering six hundred miles as I should have done for one covering twelve hundred miles, I have been urged to take one for the longer distance and get rid of it on the best terms I could for the latter part of the journey. This seems to be a recognized proceeding.

The terrible jolting and shaking of that journey from Niagara to Boston still lives in my memory in spite of many later and similar experiences. I do not wonder that car sickness is a recognized affliction and upper berths are especially to be avoided on this as well as on many other accounts.

The Pullman cars are delightful, always premising that they are sufficiently full to be steady. My unhappy experience on more than one occasion has been to form one of a miserable duet of shaking and jerking passengers, the result of an empty parlor-car. Still, under ordinary conditions most of us find such carriages extremely comfortable and even luxurious.

The gentlemen's lavatory in these cars is sufficiently large to accommodate four or five men at once, whereas that set apart for the ladies is so small that you can barely turn around in it and perform your ablutions as best you may, with a rocking, jolting motion that drives you from side to side all the time and the horrible conviction that four or five impatient or reproachful females are standing outside the door ready to take your place the moment you can be induced, by knocking or twisting at the handle, to vacate it.

Of course, when it is merely a question of one night on board washing becomes a minor consideration and can be supplemented to any extent at home or in your hotel. But the peculiar boast of the American car system is its adaptability to long railway journeys extending over several days. Having received many really well earned compliments from various sleeping-car porters on which I may call Non Lavatory Monopoly, I feel more entitled to speak on the subject than many ladies would be who spend an uncomfortable half hour in an elaborate arrangement of their bangs while some poor wretch is waiting outside for the chance of washing her hands after the long, black night journey.

In addition to greater space for toilet arrangements men have another advantage on board these cars, namely, that their clothes are much more easily taken off or put on sitting on a berth, with the board of the upper berth within two inches of the top of your head.

A DROLL PORTER

[From *The Australian in London and America*, James Francis
Hogan (London, 1889), pp. 44-46]

When 10 o'clock comes round our Negro conductor begins to bestir himself and to work out that interesting process by which our comfortably cushioned and luxuriously appointed Pullman car becomes quickly transformed into an equally comfortable and luxurious dormitory on wheels. Passengers may enter into possession of their appointed berths whenever they please, and at midnight, when all have retired and the young lady passengers have ceased to titter at the novelty of the situation, the Negro attendant turns down the lights and proceeds to improvise a bed for himself in the smoking-room at the rear of the car.

In crossing the continent one comes into contact with almost every type of Negro conductor—the serious and the humorous, the stately and the unassuming, the distant and the familiar, the talkative and the reserved. But as a rule they are very careful, obliging and attentive to their duties, and at the end of each stage it is the custom to make a little collection on their behalf, each passenger generally contributing a quarter of a dollar. Some of these sable guardians have quite an extensive budget of comical incidents stored in their memories. The one who had charge of us from Salt Lake City to Denver was wont to keep the ladies perpetually laughing at his droll stories and the still droller way he had of telling and acting them. While he was with us the beds were made up every night to a continuous accompaniment of rippling merriment.

He narrated how on one very hot and oppressively close evening a restless lady passenger, resolving to obtain coolness at any cost, violently kicked off her blankets, but in doing so she unfortunately overlooked the fact that her own clothes were stacked near the window that she had thrown open before retiring in order to admit some fresh air. Thus it was that in her struggles to cool herself she inadvertently kicked her wearing apparel out of the window, with the embarrassing result that next morning she was constrained to make her appearance airily attired in a hat, stockings and a blanket. On another occasion a male passenger of giant proportions, finding his berth too small for the length of his corporeal frame, thrust his feet through the open window as the best and most comfortable solution to the difficulty. When he awoke in the morning he found to his intense disgust that his feet had changed color during the night. They had been covered by a thick coating of tar by some roadside station humorist who, seeing them dangling out-side the window, was unable to resist the temptation.

~ 1 8 9 1 ~

AN EARLY LUXURY TRAIN

[From *A Yorkshireman's Trip to the United States and Canada*, William Smith (London, 1892), pp. 160, 161, 191]

May 14, 1891. I left Philadelphia at twelve noon by the Chicago Limited express train on the Pennsylvania line for Chicago, a distance of 822 miles. This train is timed to reach its destination at 10 A.M. the following day, the local time being one hour later than New York. It is what is called a limited train, which means that it consists of four Pullman sleeping-cars, a smoking-car, a dining-car, an observation-car and a composite-car, the last named having a compartment for luggage, a place for the mail and sleeping berths for the conductors. The smoking-car has a reading-room for the passengers, library, easy chairs, writing and card tables and a barber's shop. The traveler can have his hair cut, curled and shampooed for half a dollar, a shave for a quarter, or a bath at the rate of forty miles an hour for seventy-five cents. The cars are designated palace-cars and they fully deserve the title, for they are indeed traveling palaces where one can obtain all the comforts of home.

For ordinary traffic and short distances the cars are all alike in appearance, though special provision is made for smokers, women and children. The seats are well stuffed, covered with velvet plush and are easy to luxuriousness. The windows are made to lift and they are fitted with Venetian blinds which can be opened or shut at pleasure. The conductors who rendered me great service are smart and dignified in appearance, courteous in their behavior and what is most surprising, proof against tips, the offer of which would be regarded as an insult.

～☙

Baltimore & Ohio local, 1890 (by courtesy of the Baltimore & Ohio Railroad)

INDEX